Academic Achievement in Relation to Classroom Environment of Rural and Urban Students

Academic Achievement in Relation to Classroom Environment of Rural and Urban Students

Gouri Sharma

AUTHORSPRESS
Publishers of Creative & Scholarly Books

Worldwide Circulation through Authorspress Global Network
First Published in 2017
by
Authorspress
Q-2A Hauz Khas Enclave, New Delhi-110 016 (India)
Phone: (0) 9818049852
e-mails: authorspress@rediffmail.com; authorspress@hotmail.com
Website: www.authorspressbooks.com

Academic Achievement in Relation to Classroom Environment of Rural and Urban Students
ISBN 978-93-5207-399-3

Printed in India at Krishna Offset, Shahdara

Preface

Quality Education is one of the key factors in the national development. Education is seen as an indispensable asset for achieving the idea of peace, freedom and social justice besides being an instrument to reduce poverty, ignorance and oppression of war. There is also a need for acquiring and developing curiosity and pleasure in learning. Effective learning to a great extent depends on the way of teaching and overall atmosphere of learning. Measuring achievement is a major part of the learning process and informs educators of student talent and progress toward educational goals. Today's modern society expects each one to be a high achiever. It has become an indicator of a child's future. Parents, teachers and higher authorities concerned with effective academic achievement of the students. The reasons for achieving low in academics are numerous. It is true that in the vast majority of cases it is unable to identify the exact reason why a child is achieving low? In this context Classroom environment is seen as a major determiner of classroom behavior and learning outcome. The classroom environment has a big influence on student outcomes and plays an important role in improving the efficiency of learning in all levels of classrooms. Studies consistently have shown evidence of relations between student perceptions of their classroom learning environment and their cognitive and affective outcomes. Students learn better when they perceive their classroom environment positively. Understanding how to establish and maintain a positive classroom climate is seen as basic to improving schools. Research suggests significant relationships between classroom environment and students academic achievement. The ultimate objective of striving to work for a good classroom climate is to facilitate learning in which the students demonstrate through their active participation curiosity and attention to detail that they value the content's importance. They take obvious pride in their work and initiate improvements in it. This they do by revising drafts on their own initiative, help peers, and ensuring that high quality work is displayed. Both students and teachers establish and maintain through planning of learning activities, interactions and the classroom environment of high expectations for learning are cognitively busy place with student and teacher setting a high value on high quality work/student work being displayed and student teacher interactions characterized by teacher insistence on and student acceptance of the need for students to expand their best efforts. Both students and teachers see the content as important, and student take obvious pride in their work.

How can we organize the environment in the school and classroom so that such interactions support and enhance both teaching and learning, and where children feel safe, happy and wanted, and which teachers find meaningful and professionally satisfying? Yet not enough attention is paid to the importance of classroom environment for learning. Often classrooms are overcrowded, with no alternative spaces to learn, nor are they attractive, inviting or sensitive towards children's needs. Keeping in view the importance of classroom environment in relation to academic achievement of the rural and urban students, the present study aimed to investigate the relationship between classroom environment along with its various dimensions, locale and sex with academic achievement.

This book has been divided into six chapters. The first chapter of the book deals with the introduction part. The second chapter comprises the review of literature concerning the factors affecting academic achievement including classroom environment, providing a theoretical groundwork of the investigation. Chapter three presents the problems and hypotheses of the study. Fourth chapter describes the methodology adopted in the present study, which includes samples, tools used, design and procedure. The obtained results have been discussed in the fifth chapter. Findings of this study may have some implication in educational sector. We hope that the results of the present study would enable the parents, teachers, educational administrators and social workers in particular and the society in general. It is expected that these information would probe into a better understanding of increased awareness of the classroom psychosocial environment. Teacher support, affiliation, task orientation and involvement factors may increase the academic achievement of the students. In sum, these findings could provide useful information for those who wish to develop educational programs to improve students academic achievement.

Any accomplishment requires the blessings of the Almighty and efforts of many people; this work is the outcome of the same. The successful completion of any task would be incomplete without the expression of gratitude to all those people who have helped me throughout. It is extremely difficult to express gratitude to all those who have devoted their precious time and have provided continuous inspiration, motivation and encouragement and support to me.

The present work is the result of consistent help, guidance, and encouragement, which I received from my supervisor Dr. Meeta Jha, Professor, School of Studies in Psychology, Pt.

Ravishankar Shukla University, Raipur (C.G.). I am indebted to her for the continuous support at an every step of my research work.

I express my warmest thanks and deep sense of gratitude to Dr. B. G. Singh, Vice Chancellor, Pt. Sundarlal Sharma Open University Chhattisgarh, Bilaspur, for his generous help throughout. I express heartfelt gratitude to Dr. Mitashree Mitra, Professor and Head, School of Regional Studies & Research, Pt. Ravishankar Shukla University, Raipur (C.G.), Dr. O. P. Verma, former Professor and Head, School of Regional Studies & Research, Pt. Ravishankar Shukla University, Raipur (C.G.) for their valuable suggestions, well wishes and co-operation.

I owe my sincere thanks to the Principals and the Teachers of various Higher Secondary Schools for permitting me to collect the data from their institution. I cannot forget in extending my thanks to the respondents who provided the desired information and thus, made me ever to remain indebted to them.

I gratefully acknowledge all the Authors and Publishers, whose work assisted me in finding the base of my studies.

I would like to express my warmest thanks and deep sense of gratitude to my husband Shri. Rajeev Sharma who deserves the credit of this entire endeavor. He has been a constant source of inspiration and encouragement for this work. Indeed, words are inadequate to convey my deep sense of gratitude, thanks and appreciation to my family members, my father Shri. R.V. Gupta, my mother-in-law Smt. Rampyari Sharma, and my loving children Anushka and Rudransh for their love, obstinate sacrifice, blessings, affectionate encouragement and support throughout.

Gouri Sharma

Raipur

Contents

List of Tables

List of Graphs

List of Abbreviations

A	Affiliation
Aca. Ach	Academic Achievement
C.E	Classroom Environment
C	Competition
F	Female
I	Involvement
Inn	Innovation
M	Male
M	Mean
O&O	Order and Organization
R.C.	Rule Clarity
R	Rural
S.D.	Standard Deviation
T.C.	Teacher Control
T.O.	Task Orientation
T.S.	Teacher Support
U	Urban

1

Introduction

Nature and Concept of Academic Achievement

Achievement is one of the main factors in assessing the quality of education in a society. Identifying the factors that affect students learning and, thus, achievement continues to be an important objective of study of educators of different countries.

Achievement has been defined as the level of a person's learning and his ability to apply what he has learned. The main focus of educative process is to improve the performance or learning of the student, the learning outcomes of the students are measured with the help of their achievement.

According to Steinberger (1993) "Academic achievement generally refers to the level of success attained in some specific or general area concerning scholastic or academic work. It is a multidimensional, related to human growth and cognitive, emotional, social and physical development, it reflects the whole child and not a single instance, but occurs across time and levels, through a student's life in public school and post-secondary years and working life". Goods (1973) has defined academic achievement as a knowledge attain or skill develop in the school subject usually designate by test score or by mark assign by teachers or by both. "Achievement is reflected by the extent to which skill or knowledge has been imparted to him (Crow and Crow, 1969)."

In this competitive world, quality of performance has become the key factor for personal progress. Parents desire that their children perform as high a level as possible. This desire for a high level of achievement puts a lot of pressure on students, teachers and schools and in general the education system itself. In fact, it appears as if the whole system of education revolves round the academic achievement of students, though various other outcomes are also expected from the system thus a lot of time and effort of the schools are used for helping students to achieve better in their scholastic endeavors. The importance of scholastic and academic achievement has raised important questions for educational researchers. What factors promote achievement in students? How far do the different factors contribute towards academic achievement? (Ramaswamy, 1990).

SIGNIFICANCE OF THE STUDY

The world is changing very fast and the "modern society expects each one to be a high achiever" (Daulta, 2008,). However, success is considered history of high expectations to provide challenge and inspiration necessary to push the individual to highest level of performance (Ozturk & Debelak, 2005) and whatever the obstacles are, each one is encouraged to succeed and considered important by society members. President George W. Bush signed law on January 8, 2002, which clearly demonstrated a strong national commitment in improving the academic success of all children (U.S. Department of Education, 2002) in the No Child Left Behind (NCLB) Act of 2001. The NCLB legislation which is forcing school to focus on student outcomes, this focuses on accountability and pressurize on administrators, teachers, and school counselors. These professionals take the responsibility for making the changes that are mandated within the NCLB and are involved in the process of increasing student achievement, reducing the achievement gap, improving school attendance, graduation rates, and ensuring safety within school systems.

Quality Education is the key factor in national development. Education is asset for achieving peace, freedom and social justice besides being an instrument to limit poverty, ignorance and oppression of war. There is a need to acquire and develop curiosity and pleasure in learning. Effective learning depends on the way of teaching and overall atmosphere of learning. The Right of Children to Free and Compulsory Education (RTE) Act, 2009 emphasizes on every school and teacher to be child friendly and promote child centered teaching learning process with ample freedom of expression for every child to learn and develop to full potential. It is essential for every teacher, child and member of school management committee (SMC) to make own school and society RTE compliant, which would take care of the rights of every child irrespective of her or, his background and educational levels. This expects every concerned with the system accordingly. It calls conscious effort by everybody alarmed with children's lives. Childs learning and holistic development calls for a lot of collective efforts and a good understanding at every level of the new approach. RTE defined each indicator in a specific and measurable manner with focus on the following indicators. Every child in neighborhood studies in school, every child likes to go to school every day, every child takes active part in school's activities, every child looks happy, healthy and confident, every child learns to desired levels (whole child) every child's learning progress is recorded CC way, every teacher looks involved and happy, parents of every child take interest in school, school's enrolment and attendance touch upper mark regularly. The number of indicators looks small, but, it requires enormous efforts to achieve these for every student. RTE categorized all the parameters in five broad areas. They include Physical Environment of the school, Learning Environment, Teacher Development and Teacher Support, Learning Processes and Assessment and School Management processes.

FACTORS AFFECTING ACADEMIC ACHIEVEMENT

Academic achievement is the most significant topic in the field of educational research. Numerous studies have been carried out to bring various factors that influence academic achievement which have been hypothesized and researched upon. Investigators have come out with varied results, sometimes complementing and sometimes contradicting each other. A major part of a learners life, approximately six hours every day is spent in the classroom. The development and performance of student at school is reflected in various areas such as the academic, cultural and sporting spheres, good academic results often indicate future vocational success.

The first effort in this direction in India can be seen in the first educational research survey edited by Buch (1974, as cited in Stanley, 2005) The trend report on achievement included categories namely, correlates in general, personality correlates, socio-economic status, backwardness and failure, over and under achievement and miscellaneous (Dave, 1974). The trend report in the second survey of research in education (Dave & Anand,1979), classified studies under the same categories namely correlates in general, personality correlates, socio-economic status, backwardness and failure, over and under achievement and miscellaneous. However, the category: backwardness and failure was replaced by poor curriculum organization. The trend report in third survey of research by

Anand and Padma (1987) education classified studies on correlates of achievement under eight categories: personality, creativity and achievement, affective correlates socio-economic status and achievement, over and under achievers, achievement of SC/ST students, institutional characteristics and achievement and miscellaneous.

The trend report in the fourth survey of research in education of the studies on correlates of achievement (Padma, 1991) classified studies by (i) variable, (ii) educational level, and (iii) subjects. The variables were further analyzed under four broad categories, viz., student related, teaching related, sociological and other. The student related variable were – intelligence, anxiety, values interest and aptitudes. Teaching related variable were mostly the process variables dealing with method of teaching and classroom interaction, socio-economic status was the predominant sociological variable with home environment, parental attitude, aspiration, encouragement and cultural influences as the second level variables. In the fifth survey of research Balasubramanian (1997) has discussed three broad categories that include the cognitive variable, the affective variable, and environment that is school and home related variable as correlates of achievement. The reasons for achieving low in academics are numerous. It is true that in majority of cases it is unable to identify the exact reason of child achieving low. Research is bringing a complete understanding of the ways in which the low achieving child's psychological, social and researchers constantly lament that all the question are not answered, it is known more today about how to tackle these children then it was 10-15 years ago. A low achiever is one who is not able to use his or her innate capacities and does not show educational success, commensurate with his or her abilities. This builds up stress and tension in the child. There is a wealth of studies documenting educational attainment of students, it is thus, evident that the researches on determinants of achievement have expanded in many directions. However, the determinants that effect educational performance can be grouped into three main categories that is – (a) Personal Factor, (b) School Factor and (c) Socio Cultural Factor.

(a) Personal Factors

Personal factors include intelligence, motivation, self-concept, thinking style, study habit, anxiety, interest, level of aspiration, as the determinant of academic achievement, among which intelligence, motivation, study habit and anxiety acquire relevance.

Intelligence

Intelligence is the potential for learning something and technical skills learnt depend on the academic intelligence. Intelligence is a broad concept presumably generalizing across, many domains of human functioning. It has to do with a person's number of ways to deal with tasks involving discriminations abstractions and problem solving. According to Wechsler (1958). "The global capacity of the individual to act purposefully, think rationally and deal effectively with his emotions.

Psychologist has proposed numerous theories to articulate and explore the notion of intelligence. A number of psychometric theories of intelligence such as the two factor theory by Spearman, (1927), Thursetone's theory of primary mental abilities (1938), Vernon's hierarchical theories (1971), the structure of intellect model by Guilford (1967) and human cognition abilities (Carnol,1993), have been proposed. There had been a debate regarding the causal precedence of intelligence and academic achievement. (Watkins *et. al.,* 2007). Several researchers found significant relationships between academic achievement and intelligence (Allik & Realo, 1997; Fagan, Holland, & Wheeler, 2007; Gagne & St Pere, 2002; Koke

&Vernon, 2003; Laidra *et. al.,* 2007; Mayes & Calhoun, 2007a, 2007b; McGrew & Flanagan, 1997; Neisser *et. al.*, 1996; Rohde & Thompson, 2007; Saleh, *et. al.,* 2001; Sternberg *et. al.*, 2001; Watkins, Lei, & Canivez, 2007; and Williams *et. al.*, 2002).

Motivation

While there are a number of factors that affect performance in school, one of the most important and influential factor is motivation. Motivation, also referred as academic engagement, academic engagement is "cognitive, emotional, and behavioral indicators of students investment in and attachment to education" (Tucker, Zayco, & Herman, 2002). It is obvious that students who are less motivated to succeed will not work hard. Several researchers suggested that only motivation directly affects academic achievement; others affect achievement only through motivation (Tucker *et. al.,* 2002). It is not as easy to understand what motivate students. Numerous studies have been conducted on this topic, which led to the development of several theories of motivation. One widely accepted theory is Goal theory. It postulates that there are two main types of motivation for achieving in school. Students with an ability or performance goal orientation are concerned with proving their competence by getting good grades or performing well compared to other students (Anderman & Midgley, 1997; Maehr & Midgley, 1991). On the other hand, students with a task goal orientation are motivated by a desire to increase their knowledge on a subject or by enjoyment from learning the material. Studies have shown that students with a task goal orientation are more likely to engage in challenging tasks, seek help as needed, and adopt useful cognitive strategies, and, possibly most importantly, tend to be happier both with school and with themselves as learners (Ames, 1992; Anderman & Midgley, 1997).

Anxiety

Anxiety is a common phenomenon of everyday's life. It plays a crucial role in human life as all of us are victims of anxiety in different ways. Anxiety is either be a trait anxiety or a state anxiety. Trait anxiety is a stable characteristic of the person. State anxiety is aroused by temporary condition of the environment such as examination, punishment etc. The academic achievement of the students are affected due to increase in anxiety in the society. The fact that anxiety has increased in the society has not only affected education but also students personalities. Davis (2004) found that test-anxiety decreases span of attention, memory, concentration, and then leads to low academic performance. Masson, *et. Al.,* (2004) stated that students with high test–anxiety had poor school performance. Eysenck (2001) found test-anxiety creating irrelevant thought, decreased attention, concentration which leads to academic difficulties. When attention and concentration are impaired, it disrupts memory and will lead to low academic achievement (Chen, Li, 2000 and Sanders, 2001, cited in Needham, 2006). Rohen and Meetei (2012) stated that academic anxiety is a state anxiety which relates to impending danger from environment of academic institutions including teachers, certain subjects like Mathematics, English etc.

Study Habit

The concept of study habit combines nearly all other sub-topics such as study attitude, method and skill. Research on the correlation between study habit and students academic performance has received attention from scholars and educational agencies. Study habits are learning tendencies. Study habit can be students way of study either in systematic, efficient or inefficient manner, this definition means that efficient study habit leads to positive academic performance and inefficient study habit leads to academic failure. Study habit are measured directly through reports, examination, assessment, rating, etc. Students attitude and study habit has been described as a belief about the subject and implicit evaluative responses, one important component of learning activities is study skills. Various students have study practices based on their study habits and their interest in subject. Three distinct factors have identified which contribute to better educational achievements: 1-Competence, 2-Interest, 3-Study skills. Effective study usually comes down to two factors: motivation and style. Numerous studies have focused on various aspect of study skills to exhibit relationship between study skills and academic performance in college students viz., Ayodele & Adebiyi, 2013), Fazal, Hussain, Majaka and Massood (2012), Nandita and Tanima (2004) Novhi (2008) Onwuegbuzie, slate & schwartz (2001) Saini (2013).

Interest

Interest is also considered to be an important determinant of success in any activity. It is one of the critical constructs related to learning and so associated with academic achievement also. Interest in a subject is related to motivation and learning (Schiefele & Csikszentmihalyi, 1995). Regarding students interest in higher education, evidence abounds that interest in learning had been found to be highly correlated (0.70) with college students grades in specific courses (Lavin, 1965). More studies confirmed correlations between interest, comprehension and learning (Renninger, Hidi, Krapp, & Renninger, 1992). Literature also suggests interest in schooling predicted self-efficacy (Adeyemo, 2005); there was a significant relationship between interest and achievement (Olatoye, 2004, Olatoye & Ogunkola, 2008), students motivation levels has significantly importance to their academic achievement (Epstein & Sheldon, 2002; Hamilton, Hinton, & Qian, 2008).

Self Concept

Allport (1961) has described the self-concept as, self is something which we are aware, we think of it as the warm, central private region in our life, it plays a crucial part in our consciousness, thus, it is some kind of core in our being. Combs and Syngg (1964) refers self-concept as, "the individual's perception." It refers to perceptions, beliefs, feelings, attitudes and values which individual views as part of himself, the person abstractions, evaluations about physical abilities, physical appearance, intelligence, social skills, psychological self-image, self-confidence, self-respect and self-adequacy. Various researchers concluded that self-conceptions become differentiated, complex and better organized as individuals progress (Byrne & Shavelson, 1996; Harter, 1999; Marsh, 1989). Self-concept was defined by Shavelson *et. al.*, (1976) as "a person's perception of himself through his experience with his environment". Hence, a positive self-concept would be valued as a desirable goal across many educational settings (Australian Educational Council, 1989;). Self-concept as educational factor, research has shown that higher levels of self-concept are linked to many educational outcomes (for example, Marsh, 1990a; Marsh and Craven, 1997; Marsh and Hau, 2003). Thus, observed developmental trend is good reason in understanding academic achievement and wellbeing will be further enhanced by giving consideration to self-concept. It determines not only the kinds of goals suitable for a student to strive for, but also his aspiration level.

Level of Aspiration

Level of aspiration is another variable that affects academic performance. Every individual has goals and he/she aspires to achieve this goal. In the course of achieving this goal, one has some expectation. The standard one wants to achieve in any task is described as there level of aspiration. Level of aspiration should be high enough to be challenging and low enough to be attainable. Gardner (1940) defines, "level of aspiration as a quantitative concept, which has requirements like that the subjects make some public indication of his aims and that, it is in quantitative terms." Hurlock (1967) defined "a longing for one's achieved level with advancement on it as its end. In other words, level of aspiration is the goal an individual sets in a task, which has intense personal significance or in which ego is involved. Students educational aspirations are related to educational attainment (Hanson 1994, Horn & Carroll 1997, Wilson & Portes1975) and achievement (Astone & McLanahan, 1991, Hanson, 1994, and Jencks, Crouse & Mueser, 1983).

(b) School Factors

School factors include all the variables directly connected with school such as classroom environment, student teacher relationship, teacher support teaching technique etc.

The school determinants constitute the more recent research on academic achievement which has helped in the identification of variables and school operating patterns associated with students performance as well as a more positive environment for learning. At the school level, the determinants of achievement include the physical environment, psychosocial environment of the classroom, teaching methods and teacher student relationship, teacher education. In the present study classroom environment taken as the independent variable for determining the academic achievement of the students.

Classroom Environment

Classroom is "home away from home" for you and your students. Make it attractive, comfortable, and functional (Young, 2002). It includes a broad range of educational concepts, physical setting, psychological environment through social contexts, and instructional components related to teacher characteristics also behavior. The study has been widespread across all sub specializations of educational psychology. Taking a cue from definitions offered by expert's classroom climate could be defined as a set of characteristics that describe a classroom, differentiate it from other classrooms and effect the behavior of teachers and students in it, enduring over a period of time (Halpin & Croft, 1963). As school environment has been found related to the performance of the school, particularly of teachers, classroom environment has been found related to the performance of students in a particular classroom (Sharma 1982).

One suggested taxonomy of 'organizational' climate comprises four categories; ecology, milieu, social system and culture. The ecological construct describes the physical and material environment of the classroom and school. Milieu describes the characteristics of individuals at each level. Social system includes patterns and rules of government as well as nature of relationships amongst and between pupils and staff. Work culture depicts norms and values prevalent in the class or the school as an organization. All these put together, depict the ethos of the school, ultimately, good classroom climate or environment is the one which moves towards good work culture in the class as well as a whole; also, school wide commitment to the culture greatly strengthens the classroom environment. Such a climate works for creating an environment of respect and rapport with themselves. It starts with teachers demonstrating genuine caring and respect for individual students. The ideal of common school advocated by the Kothari Commission (1964-66) five decades ago continues to be valid as it reflects the values enshrined in our Constitution. Schools will succeed in inculcating these values only if they create an ethos in which every child feels happy and relaxed. This ideal is even more relevant now because education has become a fundamental right, which implies that millions of first-generation learners are being enrolled in schools.

The ultimate objective of striving to work for a good classroom climate is to facilitate learning in which their active participation curiosity and attention in detail that they value the content's importance. They take obvious pride in work and initiate improvements. Which they do by revising drafts on their own initiative, help peers, and ensure high quality work. Both students and teachers establish and maintain through planning of learning activities, interactions and the classroom environment of high expectations for learning are cognitively busy place with student and teacher setting a higher value on higher quality work. Student work being displayed and student teacher interactions characterized by teacher insistence and student acceptance, the need for students to expand their best efforts. Students and teachers see the content as important, and student take obvious pride in their work.

How can we organize the environment in the school and classroom that such interactions support and enhance teaching and learning? How can the space in the school be nurtured where children feel safe, happy and wanted, which teachers find meaningful and professionally satisfying? Children are constantly interacting with the physical environment of their schools during structured or unstructured time, consciously or unconsciously. Not enough attention is given to the importance of physical environment for learning. Often classrooms are overcrowded, no alternative spaces to learn, nor attractive, inviting or sensitive towards children's needs. Inappropriate school design may drastically affect the teacher's productive output and classroom management. In fact, the role of this all-encompassing, physical environment has been restricted merely to shelter the educational activity (NCF 2005).

The concept of classroom climate implies in establishing and maintaining a positive context which facilitates learning, but in practice, classroom climates range from hostility or toxic to welcoming and supportive. It can fluctuate daily and over the school year, because the concept is a social psychological construct, different observers can have different perceptions of the climate in a classroom, Moos (1979) measured classroom environment as shared perceptions. Fraser (1998) and Freiberg (1999) mentioned prevailing approaches to measuring classroom climate uses teacher and student, external observer's ratings and systematic coding, naturalistic inquiry, ethnography, case study, and assessment techniques.

Classroom climate is seen as a major determiner of classroom behavior, learning, and understanding to establish and maintain positivity is seen as basic to improving schools. Research suggested significant relationships between classroom climate and matters like student engagement, behavior, self'-efficacy, achievement, social and emotional development, leadership, educational reform, burnout, and quality of school life. Studies report strong associations between achievement and classrooms are perceived as having cohesion and goal-direction, less disorganization and conflict. Research suggested that the impact of classroom may be greater on students from low-income homes and groups often are discriminated against. Given the nature of classroom climate research, cause and effect interpretations remain speculative. The broader body of research on organizational climate does suggest that increasing demands for higher achievement test scores and reliance on social and tangible rewards to control behavior and motivate performance contribute to a classroom environment that is reactive and over-controlling (Mahony & Hextall, 2000).

Classroom climate has been ever changing. The elements of climate have been complex, ranging from the quality of interactions to the physical comfort levels of the individuals. No single factor has determined climate, however, the interaction of various factors have created a fabric of support that may have affected learning at optimum levels. Making even small changes in the classroom has been thought to lead to significant improvements in climate (Bolender, 1997) but determining the specific changes impacting climate and resulting in improved student achievement has been difficult to determine.

The concept of school effectiveness has been of significant, since the 1970s. Effective school correlations were identified, and one of these correlates was safe and orderly climate (Bolender, 1997.as cited in Benett (2001). The concept of a learning environment has been since the 1930s. Lewin and Murray (as cited in Fraser, 1981) presented theoretically points recognizing both environment and its interaction with personal characteristics of as the determinants of human behavior. Conceptualization of classroom climate was derived from social psychology literature and rooted in Murray's (1938) model, Getzels and Thelen's (1960) notion of classroom as social system, and Walberg's (1971) model of classroom environments.

In Murray's model (as cited in Fraser, 1981), the learning environment conceptualized as complex of environmental press, related to a corresponding complex of personal needs. Murray introduced "alpha press" to describe the environment assessed by a detached observer, and beta press" to describe the environment as perceived by milieu inhabitants. Stern's (1970) Person-Environment Congruence Theory, based on Murray's model, proposed more congruence between personal needs and environmental press leading to enhancing outcomes. By following Murray's, Getzels and Thelen's model suggested that within classes, personality, roles and climates interacted as well as predicted group behaviors, including learning. Climate developed the way in which role requirements and personality needs were balanced (Deng, 1992). The goal-behaviors of one geared into the other related social systems, within the class, goal-behavior was achieved through integration of institutions, definition of roles, and setting of expectations for the performance of relevant tasks, in performing the role-behaviors expected, the teacher taught; the students learned (Getzels & Thelen, 1960 and in Walberg's Model, (1971) (as cited in Benett, 2001) environments were linked with students aptitudes and the type of instruction to predict learning outcomes. Walberg argued about the variance in students performance was attributed to aptitude of learners and environments, with minor accounted by other variables. Nielsen and Kirk (1974), Murray's model (1938), Getzel and Thelen's model (1960), and Walberg's model (1971) gave definitions of classroom climate and generated theories about relationships of climate, antecedent and variables. Through use of theoretical models, classroom climate has focused primarily on "psychosocial environment" (Deng, 1992). Walberg (as cited in Deng, 1992) defined psychosocial environment as "the atmosphere of class as social group which potentially influences students learning". Both school effectiveness and earlier quality of school life studies employed social climate to explain the student's outcome and environmental relationship. According to Macintosh, (1991), effective schools have a critical mass of positive characteristics, when found together, accounted for differences in students achievement. The combined effect was powerful than any individual factor, and the variables were subjected to manipulation. The resulting institutional phenomenon was ethos of school climate. The notion of climate stimulated renewed interest in psycho-sociological dimension of schools among an increasing number of researchers interested in creating effective schools.

Kowalski and Reitzug (as cited in Dietrich & Bailey, 1996) took a more specific approach in the definition of climate. They defined climate as "a comprehensive structure made up of culture, physical plant, organizational structure, social relationship, and individual behavior" This definition implied that climate fluctuating rather than static, influenced by changes in outside forces as well as by the emotions of the students staff members. To create a positive climate, teacher had to be aware of changes and also had to be flexible in dealing with them (Dietrich & Bailey, 1996). Over the past several decades research has firmly established classroom learning environment as a thriving field of study (Deng, 1992; Edmonds & Federiken, 1979; Fraser; 1981; Walberg, 1979). Climate could positively influence the health of the learning environment, or it could significantly impede learning. Thus, feedback about climate could play an important role in reform (Freiberg, 1998). Anderson (1982) argues that the following classroom climate factors influence academic achievement at schools: The physical environment of the classroom for example, its size relates to learner space; the social system (relationships and interactions between learners and relationships and interactions between learners and their educators which relates to learner involvement) and learner behavior in classrooms (i.e. discipline). The impact of classroom climate on students and staff can be beneficial or barrier to learning, classroom climate is perceived quality of setting. It emerges in a fluid state from complex transaction of immediate environmental factors like physical, material, organizational, operational, and social variables. Key concepts related to understanding classroom climate include social system organization, social attitudes, staff and student morale, power, control, guidance, support, and evaluation structures, curricular and instructional practices, communicated expectations, efficacy, accountability demands, cohesion, competition, the "Fit" between key learner and classroom variables, system maintenance, growth, and change, orderliness, and safety. Moos (1979) groups concepts into three dimensions for classifying human environments and used them to develop measures of school and classroom climate, These dimensions are Relationship dimension, Personal development dimension, System maintenance and change dimension.

(i) *Relationship dimension*: The nature and intensity of personal relationships within the environment-, the extent to which people are involved in the environment, support and help each other.

(ii) *Personal development dimension*: basic directions along with personal growth and self enhancement tend to occur.

(iii) *System maintenance and change dimension*: the extent to which the environment is orderly, clear, maintains control, and responsive to change.

Moos and Trickett (1974) have identified nine important areas under above mentioned three dimensions of classroom environment which can be identified in a classroom environment they are interdependent yet, like the various branches of a tree; they constitute the tree as a whole. They tend to influence the direct and indirect impact of school environment on the educational and social development of the students. There are as under:-

(i) *Involvement (I):* Measures the extent to which student have attentive interest in the class activities and participate in discussion. Learning is an active process, it presupposes active involvement by the learner in the act of learning before it can take place (Nicholsan & Lucas, 1984). As a result of active involvement learners learn what they are expected to learn to their fullest potential. In a positive classroom climate learners are happy and enjoy going to school, and educators work together in a systematic way to achieve their objectives (Chrispeels, 1992). Research evidence in the United States has suggested that student academic involvement is a powerful predictor of their achievement. Hong and Lee (2000), Rao, Moely and Sachs (2000), Wentzel (1993); have shown that student academic engagement is positively associatiated with their achievement outcome. Astin's student involvement theory supports actively engaging students in education (Huttey, 2004). Thus academic achievement of learners is influenced either positively or negatively by their learning contexts. Steyn (2001) stated that learner involvement, support, encouragement are important factors influencing success.

(ii) *Affiliation (A):* Affiliation assess the level of friendship students feel for each other i.e. the extent to which they help each other with homework get to know each other easily, and enjoy working together. Student's relations within classroom were related to students academic progress. Lubbers, (2006) studied the impact of peer relations on academic progress and found that those who were accepted by peers had lower possibility to retain a grade or to move down.

Adolescents spend lot of time with their peers during each school day, which is reasonable as they influence each other's academic engagement and achievement. Researcher revealed that peers affect all facts of a student's life, especially social and emotional adjustment, educational aspirations and day to day behavior in school for example Berndt, 1999; Fuligni, Eccles, Barber and Clements, 2001; Steinberg, Dornbusch and Brown, 1992, found that peer influence peaks during adolescence.

(iii) *Teacher Support (TS):* Teacher support measures the amount of help, concern and friendship the teacher directs toward the students. The teacher plays a vital role in creating a climate that supports effective teaching and learning in the classrooms Thus the organization of learning space, learner involvement and discipline in the classroom are important factors influencing academic achievement quality is at the top of the agendas of educational policy makers and improving quality is probably the most important task facing educational institutions today. Increased quality of education makes the difference between success and failure. Educators play important role in development of learners and research says that both learners and parents regard educators as one of the important factors influencing success of the learners. In this regard, organization of learning space, learner involvement and discipline in the classroom play a major role in influencing academic achievement. The quality of social and emotional interaction in a classroom between and among students and teachers. Creates the CEC (Pianta *et. al.,* 2008) the literature suggests that teachers who create a healthy classroom emotional climate are likely to foster students feelings of connectedness on positive student-teacher relationships and, in turn, better classroom behavior. Teacher support refers that teachers care about students, value and establish personal relationships (e.g., Fraser &Fisher, 1982; Goodenow, 1993; Trickett & Moos, 1973). Researchers suggest positive associations between perceptions of teacher support, students adaptive motivational beliefs and engaged behavior. When students view teacher to be supportive they report higher interest, valuing, effort, and enjoyment in school work (Midgley *et. al.,* 1989; Trickett & Moos, 1974), a positive self-concept (Felner, Aber, Primavera, & Cauce, 1985), and greater expectancies for success (Goodenow, 1993). Perceiving a teacher to be supportive is related to asking help with school work when needed (Newman & Schwager, 1993).

(iv) *Task Orientation (TO):* Task Orientation measure the extent to which it is important to complete the activities that have been planned. Research suggested that student academic engagement is a significant predictor of their academic achievement (Wentzer, 1993). Students academic engagement is positively associated with their achievement outcomes (Hong & Lee, 2000; Rao, Moely, & Sachs, 2000). Hong and Lee found that high achieving group were more self-motivated, persistent and responsible in doing their homework than low achieving group.

(v) *Competition (C):* One extremely important consideration in the development of classroom climate was that of cooperation verses competition. A proper approach combining cooperation and competition in fostering student learning serves students to achieve academic success on their team and on an individual basis within the team (Ediger, 1996) Competition assesses the emphasis placed on student competing with each other for grades recognition. Coakley (1994) defined Competition as a process that socially occurs when rewards are given to people on their performances compared with others doing the same task or same event. Graham, (1976) stated that the three forms of competition that is direct, indirect, and cooperative hold positive and negative components. Cooperation includes potentially positive and negative aspects. It has been defined by (Coakley, 1994) as "a social process by which performance is evaluated and rewarded in terms of collective achievements of group of people working together to reach a particular goal".

(vi) *Order and Organization (O & O):* Assesses the emphasis on students behaving in an orderly, polite manner and on the overall organization of assignment and also classroom activity. The degree to which student tend to remain calm and quit is consider.

(vii) *Rule Clarity (RC):* Rule Clarity assesses the emphasis on establishing and following set of rules and knowing the extent to which teacher is consistent in dealing with students who break rules.

(viii) *Teacher Control (TC):* Teacher control measure how strict the teacher is in enforcing the ruler and the severity of the punishment for rules in fraction. Appropriate dominance has identified studies discussed by Marzano and Marzano as characteristic of effective teacher-student relationships (Wubbels *et. al.*, 1999; Wubbels & Levy, 1993).

Dominance can be defined as teacher's ability providing purpose and guidance regarding both academics and student behavior. Which is negative connotation of dominance or command over others. Marzano and Marzano (2003) noted other studies indicating about their preferences for teacher behavior, students express a desire for this type of teacher-student interaction. For example interviews with more than 700 students of 4-7 grades, students showed a clear preference for strong teacher guidance and control rather permissive types of behavior (Tulley & Chiu, 1995). Teachers exhibit right dominance by clear behavior expectations, learning goals and exhibiting assertive behavior, well-ordered classrooms and schools facilitate effective teaching and good behavior management skills are necessary for teachers to perform the main task of improving learning outcome. Classroom discipline that promotes academic achievement reflects learner behavior that is not disruptive and does not interfere with the activities of the lesson. Classroom management strategies indicate that educators act according to code of conduct of the school when learners break rules and they endeavor to understand learners behavior and provide support. Learners in orderly classrooms are extremely motivated, providing positive feedback, verbal support and praise are four distinct perceived classroom control styles were determined, on the basis of balance between teacher and student control over learning.

(ix) *Innovation(Inn):* Measure how much student contributes to planning classroom activities and the amount of unusual and varying activities and assignment planned by teacher, the extent to which teacher attempts to use new techniques and encourages creative thinking in the students is considered.

(c) Socio-Cultural Factor

Relationship between family status and academic achievement of children is well established in sociological research. It has been widely documented that the academic achievement of students is linked to a number of socio-cultural variables. Among the sociocultural variables associated with academic achievement are the educational and occupational attainment levels of parents, family income and composition, ethnic and language minority status, and the absence of learning material in the home (Arias, 1986; Rumberger, 1983, Steinberge, Blinde, Chan, 1984). Social class has a significant effect on the academic achievement (Taj, 1999; Van Laar & Sidarians, 2001), Researches suggest that high status of families help in achievement and provide better psychological support of their children (Williams, 1987; Williams, Lony, Carpenter and Hayden, 1993). The findings by Okpala, Okpala and Smith (2001) support the notion that economic circumstances are correlated with academic achievement.

(i) *Sex:* Sex refers biological status of a person and categorized as male, female, or intersex and gender means the attitudes, feelings, and behaviors that a given culture associates with a person's biological sex. There has been evidence of ever increasing gender gap in educational achievement. (Fergusson & Horwood, 1997; Hillman & Rothman, 2003; Praat, 1999; Thiessen &

Nickerson,1999; Weaver-Hightower, 2003). May be males have traditionally out performed females in mathematics and science, this advantage appears to be not appearing (Benbow & Stanley, 1980; Hyde, Fennema & Lamon, 1990; Hyde & Linn, 2006; Spelke, 2005). Previous research showed gender is a significant predictor of classroom perceptions. A pattern of girls perceive classroom environment positively compared to boys (e.g., Fraser & Chionh, 2000; Lawrenz, 1987). Fisher, Den Brok and Rickards's (2006) studied in Australian high schools revealed that, boy's perceived teachers to be less cooperative. Koul and Fisher (2006) studied the effect of gender on classroom environment where they employed the questionnaire on teacher interaction (Wubbels & Levy, 1993) and What Is Happening in the survey (Fraser & Chionh, 2000). Female students reported significant higher levels of leadership, helping/friendly, understanding, cohesiveness, task orientation, cooperation, and equity, and lower level of uncertainty, dissatisfaction, and admonishing. The description of these scales clearly indicates that females perceive the classroom environment more positively compared to males.

(ii) *Parental Education:* Many factors influence academic achievement beyond child's innate ability, the neighborhoods children, quality of the school, parent's education, income of the family etc., all these have an effect. According to National Institute of Health, the education of a parent is the significant predictor of a child's achievements and behavior. Probably most prominent and direct explanation of link between parent's education and children's academic achievement relies on the assumption that parents learn something during schooling which influences the way they interact with their children (Crowny & Bradley 2002, Pamela & Kean 2005, Hoff, Laursen & Tardif 2002).

(iii) *Socioeconomic Status (SES):* is evaluated as combination of factors including income, education, and occupation. It is way of looking at individuals or families fitting into society using economic and social measures that have an impact on indivuals health and wellbeing. Socioeconomic status and health are closely related, and it can have profound effects on a person's health due to differences in ability to access health care, dietary and other life style choices associated with finances and education.

(iv) Significant studies suggested socioeconomic status as the best predictor of student achievement (Coleman, *et. al.,* 1966; Lee, Bryk, & Smith, 1993). The educational status of parents is the most stable aspects of Socio Economic Status (SES) as it typically established at early age and remains same over time (Sirin, 2005). It's well documented that family plays a meaningful role in a child's academic performance and development (Cornell & Grossberg, 1987; Thompson, Alexander, & Entwisle, 1988; Tucker, Harris, Brady, & Herman, 1996). Mothers' education and family income influences adolescent's educational outcome and expectancy beliefs (Rhea & Otto, 2001). A study by Campbell, Hombo, and Mazzeo (1 999) using NAEP data indicates that students who reported higher parental education levels tend to have higher average scores. Factors in the family background have some associations with students success and in young adults' eventual educational and occupational attainment. Such variables include family structure (socioeconomic status and intact/single parent families), parents education level, their involvement and parenting style (Jacob and Harvey, 2005). Educated parents assume to create environment that facilitate proper learning (Williams, 1980; Teachman, 1987) and involve in their children's school experiences and environments (Steinberg *et. al.,* 1992, Useem, 1992). There are students from low-income and single parent are high achievers and students from high socio-economic and intact families are low achievers. Students also come from homes where parents are from high education and involved, yet achieve poorly at school (Jacob and Harvey, 2005).

(v) *Locale:* Locale is a demographic variable consider under the category of social variable in this study. People inhabit in different parts of the world and lead various types of lives. Their lifestyle change across the various region of this world and so do their thought processes. people all over the world have been divided into two distinct group is, classified as rural or urban depending on the density of human created structure and resident people in a particular area. Researchers found that locale have a direct impact on their way of living. Boylan and Mcswan (1978); Obe (1984); Edington and Martellaro (1984); Blackwell and McLaughlin(1999); Roscigno and Crowley (2001); Owoeye (2002); kshreersagar (2008); Usha (2007);

Rationale

The world is changing very fast and the "modern society expects each one to be a high achiever" (Daulta, 2008). However, "success is considered history of high expectations to provide challenge and inspiration necessary to push the individual to highest level of performance" (Ozturk & Debelak, 2005) and whatever the obstacles are, each one is encouraged to succeed and considered important by society members

It is matter of moral and intellectual strength that we find indications of enhancement and encouragement of learning needs and potentiality of children from the marginalized communities in important policy documents mainly NCF and RTE. The Eleventh Plan document, there are indications of making inclusive classrooms and work on happenings in classrooms. It is recognized now that there is a need to focus on the learning needs and quality education for children to realize the goal of quality education in India.

Keeping the needs of learners, several civil society organizations have developed teaching learning program that certainly are part of the initiative to make classrooms inclusive. This innovativeness contributes in enriching and deepening the outlook in making classrooms inclusive, by considering the needs and potentialities of the learners. For this, we have to be aware that these are context-specific and to replicate them goes against the interests of learners. We should be cautious enough about the "standardization of context-specific innovations" in the field of teaching and learning and making classrooms inclusive and democratic.

We will be unable to attain the goals and expectations in school education if we do not move ahead to address reforms in the classroom processes, paying attention to the contemporary changing realities, needs and potentialities of the learners in India. School is not just a building where children assemble, but a space where they enjoy learning life skills and the art of negotiating the self, other and the world. The desired achievements, therefore, will be based on the extent to which the needs and potentialities of the learners are addressed in the classroom and how the overall experience of learning is made joyful for these children. The benefits derived from information regarding climate and academic achievement could lead to identification of strategies that schools could take in designing effective interventions to produce improved academic performance in students. Considering the potential significance of information regarding classroom climate, attention should be given to its continued investigation. Examination of the relationship between academic achievement and classroom environment has proven to be vital, yet these has been very little current in this area specifically in Chhattisgarh state in rural and urban context. Present study was planned to investigate the relationship between academic achievement and classroom environment.

2

Review of Literature

The review of related literature is an important part of any scientific research. A review of related literature provides the researchers an insight into the problem that the investigator is going to undertake. It also helps in determining objectives and formulating hypothesis. Therefore, the main objective of a review of related literature is to have an understanding of the trends of research in the field and about the gaps in research if any. In this chapter an attempt is made to survey the earlier works done in India and abroad. These studies will help the investigator in planning and the following chapter provides a review of the literature on factors that can affect academic achievement. There are number of studies relating to the academic achievement done in the past.

The study of academic achievement is one of the most significant topics in the field of educational research. There is a range of factors that affect the quality of performance of students (Waters & Marzano, 2006). Over the past several decades research has firmly established classroom learning environment as a thriving field of study (Deng, 1992; Edmonds & Federiken, 1979; Fraser; 1981; Walberg, 1979). Climate could positively influence the health of the learning environment, or it could significantly impede learning. Thus, feedback about climate could play an important role in reform (Freiberg, 1998). The benefits derived from information regarding climate and academic achievement could lead to identification of strategies that schools could take in designing effective interventions to produce improved academic performance in students. Considering the potential significance of classroom environment, attention should be given to its continued investigation, thus there is need to examine the relationship between academic achievement and classroom environment has proven to be vital, and there is lack of study in this field specifically in the rural and urban area of Chhattisgarh State.

The first effort in this direction in India can be seen in the first educational research survey (as cited in Stanley, 2005) studied by Buch (1974). The trend report on achievement included categories namely, correlates in general, personality correlates, socio-economic status, backwardness and failure, over and under achievement and miscellaneous (Dave, 1974). The trend report in the second survey of research in education (Dave & Anand,1979), classified studies under the same categories namely correlates in general, personality correlates, socio-economic status, backwardness and failure, over and under achievement and miscellaneous. However, the category: backwardness and failure was replaced by poor curriculum organization. The trend report in third survey of research in education classified studies on correlates of achievement under eight categories: personality creativity and achievement, affective correlates, socio-economic status and achievement, over and under achievers, achievement of SC/ST students, institutional characteristics and achievement and miscellaneous (Anand & Padma, 1987). In the fourth survey of research in education, studies on correlates of achievement classified by Padma, (1991) namely (i) variable, (ii) educational level, (iii) subjects. The variables were further analyzed under four broad categories, *viz.*, student related, teaching related, sociological and other. Student related variable were intelligence, anxiety, values, interest and aptitudes etc. Teaching related variable were mostly the process variables dealing with method of teaching and classroom interaction. Socio-economic status was the predominant sociological variable with home environment, parental attitude, aspiration, encouragement and cultural influences as the second level variables. Other variables included language ability and homework. In the fifth survey of research by Balasubramanian (1997) has discussed broad categories that include the cognitive variables, the affective variables and environment (School and Home) related variables as correlates of achievement.

There is a wealth of studies documenting, educational attainment of students in other countries also. It is thus, evident that the researches on determinants of achievement have expanded in many directions. However the factors that affect academic achievement can be grouped into three main categories:

(i) *Personal factors* – which include intelligence, motivation, self-concept, study habit, anxiety, interest, level of aspiration etc.

(ii) *School factors* – includes school environment, classroom environment, teacher education, student-teacher relationship, teacher support, teaching method etc.

(iii) *Socio-cultural factors* – includes family environment, parental education, socio economic status, parental involvement.

1. Personal Factors

Researches on the personal factors of academic achievement takes currently into account of individual variables, among which intelligence, motivation, self-concept, study habit, anxiety, interest acquire relevance. These variables along with some other variable are discussed below:

Intelligence

(i) Smith, Smith and Dobbs (1991) studied relationship between vocabularies Test revised; wide range achievement and Wechsler Intelligence Scale for Children (WISC) revised and found that high correlation exist between intelligence and scholastic achievement. Several researchers examined the relationships between academic achievement and intelligence (Allik & Realo 1997; Gagne & St Pere 2002; Saleh, I. Al. *et. al.* 2001; Kossowska 1999; Kobal & Musek 2001; Koke & Vernon 2003) and found positive relationship between intelligence and academic achievement. Harris (2004) studied about measured intelligence, achievement, openness to experience and creativity and found that achievement had small to moderate positive correlations with an intelligence factor.

Colom and Mendoza (2006) studied the intelligence predicts scholastic achievement irrespective of SES factors in Brazil and found that intelligence does predict the children differences in scholastic achievement. The results emphasized personal intelligence as a genuine predictor of individual differences in scholastic achievement.

(ii) Laidra, Pullman and Allik (2007) studied the personality and intelligence as predictors of academic achievement in a large sample of 3618 students (1746 boys and 1872 girls) in Estonia. Intelligence as measured by the Raven's Standard Progressive Matrices was found to be the best predictor of students grade point average (GPA) in all grades.

(iii) Deary, Strand, Smith, and Fernandes, (2007) examined the relationship between intelligence and educational achievement and found strong correlation between intelligence and academic achievement.

(iv) Rohd and Thompson (2007) studied predicting academic achievement with cognitive ability and found that the measures of general cognitive ability continued to add to the prediction of academic achievement Further, the studies of Fraine, Damme and Onghena (2007) Ehrmann and Massey (2008) told that students having higher intelligence are high achievers in academic performance than the students having low intelligence.

(v) Habibollah *et. al.,* (2009) studied gender difference in creative perceptions of under graduate students and found that there is no significant relationship between academic achievement and intelligence. Royce (2009) studied on the grade integrity and the representation of academic achievements and found that the student's academic achievement is to some extent affected by the grade integrity Steinmayr *et. al.*, (2010) studied that do intelligence and sustained attention interact in predicting academic achievement and found that intelligence serves as significant predictors to academic achievement. Naderi (2010) studied intelligence and academic achievement: an investigation of gender differences and found that the relationship between intelligence and academic achievement is complex. It may vary by gender and by the intelligence measure used.

(vi) Mudasir and Yatu (2012) studied a comparative study of intelligence and academic achievement of Kashmiri and

Tibetan students and found significant mean differences between the two groups under investigation.

Anxiety

The academic achievements of the students are badly affected due to rise in anxiety in the society. There is no denying to the fact that anxiety has increased in the society. It is not only affects education but also students personalities which remain the whole time their lives.

Eysenck (2001) found that test-anxiety creates irrelevant thoughts, preoccupation, and decreased attention and concentration thus, leads to academic difficulties. When attention and concentration are impaired, this will disrupt memory and as a result will lead to low academic achievement (Needham, 2006).

Hancock (2001) studied effect of test anxiety and evaluation threats on students achievement and motivation at post-secondary level and found statistically significant results that student with high anxiety level performed poorly and was less motivated to learn.

Cassady and Johnson (2002) studied cognitive test anxiety and academic performance and found that anxiety exerts a significant stable and negative impact on academic performance measures. Davis (2004), found that test-anxiety decreases attention span, memory and concentration, then leads to low academic performance. Masson *et.al.,* (2004) found that high school students with high test-anxiety had a poor school performance. Chepell *et. al.,* (2005) studied text anxiety and academic performance in under graduate and graduate students and found negative relationship between test anxiety and academic achievement.

Nicholson, (2009) studied the effect of test anxiety on student achievement of grade 11 students, and found that anxiety and achievement are related to each other. Khalid and Hasan (2009) studied about text anxiety in high and low achievers, and found vice-versa relationship.

Oludipe (2009) studied influence of test anxiety on performance level on numerical tasks of secondary school physics students and found that low test anxious students performed better than high test anxious students on both numerical and non-numerical tasks in physics.

Eysenk (2009) studied the effect of anxiety on academic performance and he suggested that "A lot of the negative effects of anxiety appear to be caused by difficulties with controlling attention. This suggest that training techniques designed to enhance attention control the ability to ignore distractions and to switch attention from one task to another – could help anxious students to achieve their academic potential.

Rana and Mahmood (2010) studied the relationship between test anxiety and academic achievement and found that test anxiety is one of the factors which are responsible for student's achievement and low performance but, it can be managed by appropriate training of students in dealing with factor causing test anxiety.

Yousefi *et. al.,* (2010) examine the relationship between Test-Anxiety and academic achievement among Iranian Adolescents and found that there is a significant correlation between test anxiety and academic achievement among adolescents. In addition, there is a significant difference of academic achievement between male and female adolescents whereby female score higher in their academic achievement. It is suggested that academic achievement be improved in school settings with hold up strategies such as educational guidance, counseling and other psycho-educational program such as teaching life skill.

Al-Qaisy (2011) studied the relationship of depression and anxiety in academic achievement among group of university students and found that females are more anxious than males, while males are more depressed than females. Additionally, the result indicates that there is positive relationship between achievement and anxiety, while a negative relationship is found with depression. Rohen Meetei,(2012) stated that academic anxiety is a kind of state anxiety which relates to the imminent danger from the environment of the academic institutions including teachers, certain subjects like Mathematics, English etc..

Nadeem, Ali, Maqbool and Zaidi (2012) studied impact of anxiety on the academic achievement of students having different mental abilities at university level in Bahawalpur, Pakistan and found that with the increase in anxiety academic achievement decreases both in male and female students.

Motivation

An ambiance or environment that nurtures the motivation to learn can be cultured in the home, in the classroom, or, at a broader level, during an entire school. Much of the recent research on educational motivation has rightly centered on the classroom, where the greater part of learning takes place and where students are most likely to acquire a strong motivation to gain new knowledge (Ames 1987, Brophy 1987, Tucker, Zayco & Herman, 2002, Wlodkowski & Jaynes 1991).

Bank and Finalpson (1980) studied successful motivation of students in academic activities and found that successful students were significantly higher motivation for achievement than unsuccessful students. Motivation is the key not only to effective learning but also to good discipline. It is expected that educators will involve learners in learning activities so that effective learning can occur, but de-motivated learners will not become involved. Pretorius (1998) found that lack of motivation can lead to school fatigue, bunking, leaving school, underachievement and problem behavior.

Tella (2007) studied the impact of motivation on student's academic achievement and learning outcomes in mathematics among secondary school students in Nigeria and found that gender difference were significant when impact of motivation on academic achievement was compared in male and female students. When extent of motivation was taken as variable of interest on academic achievement in mathematics significant difference seen.

Kusarkar, *et al.,* (2011) examine how motivation affect academic performance data on motivation, study strategy and effort was collected 383 medical University students, Medical Center, Amsterdam and their academic performance results were obtained from the student administration. Structural equation modeling analysis techniques was used. A structural equation modeling analysis revealed that motivation positively correlated with academic performance through deep strategy towards study and higher study effort.

Study Habit

National Assessment of Educational Progress (NAEP) in 1994 conducted research to find out the relationship between study habits and academic achievement. The findings of this research revealed a positive correlation between study habits and academic achievement of elementary and secondary school students.

Onwuegbuzie, Slate, & Schwartz, (2001) conducted a series of studies to find out the relationship between study habits and academic success, and reported a positive relationship between them.

Nandita and Tanima (2004) conducted a study to find a relationship between study habits and attitude towards studies with academic achievement in Geography. This study was conducted using secondary school students in the 9th class in schools in Bhadrak, a district of Orissa in India. The coefficients of correlation were calculated between the variables: study habits, attitude towards study and academic achievement in Geography. It was found that there existed a positive significant relationship between attitude towards studies and academic achievement and between study habits and attitude towards studies.

Karim and Hassan (2006) studied reading habits and attitude in the digital age Analysis of gender and academic program differences in Malaysia and found that the exponential growth of digital information changes the way students perceive study material, affects reading and how printed materials are used to facilitate study.

Novhi (2008) studied about study habit and skills and academic achievement of students in Kerman University of Medical Science and found significant correlation between study skill and academic achievement. He stated that study skill is one important factor determining academic achievement of students. We must replace in effective models and habit of study with more fruitful skill in order to gain better learning.

Nuthana and Yenagi, (2009) studied the influence of study habits, self-concept on academic achievement of boys and girls and found significant relationship with achievement.

Gurubasappa (2009) studied intelligence and self-concept as correlates of academic achievement of secondary school students with the objective to find out the relationship between academic achievement with intelligence and self-concept by taking a sample of 400 students and found that there was high significant correlation between academic achievement with intelligence and self-concept; there was significant difference in the academic achievement of students with different levels of intelligence and self-concept; there was significant difference in the academic achievement of students in context of gender, type of school, medium of instruction, locality and socio economic status.

Ahmad, Hamid and Ganaie (2012) studied self-concept, level of aspiration and academic achievement of physically challenged and normal students at secondary level in district Barramullah. Results of the study highlight that the normal secondary school students have high real self-concept, level of aspiration and academic achievement as compared to physically challenged students. On the other hand, physically challenged students were found to have high ideal self as compared normal student.

Fazal, Hussain, Majaka and Massood (2012) studied the role of study skills in academic achievement of students and found significant relationship of time management skills, reading and note-taking skills with academic achievement.

Oluwatimimilehim and Owoyele (2012) studied about study habits and academic achievement in core subjects among junior secondary school students ONDO State Nigeria. They found that all the study habits' subscales, teacher 'Consultation' was most influential while the time allocation exercise, concentration, note taking reading and assignments were regarded as less integral to students academic performance.

Ayodele (2013) studied study habits as influence of academic performance of university undergraduates in Nigeria and found that faculty is a significant determinant of undergraduates study habit. Gender has been found not to influence the determinants of undergraduates' study habit.

Saini (2013) studied academic achievement of scheduled caste secondary school students in relation to study habit, home environment and school environment and found no significant relationship between study habit and academic achievement. Home environment had significant effect on academic achievement. School environment does not play a significant role in academic achievement.

Level of Aspiration

Level of aspiration is another variable that affects academic achievement. Singh (1983) studied the effect of level of aspiration on achievement and found that rural students received lower marks than urban students and there was a positive correlation between level of aspiration and achievement.

Abu Hilal (2000) studied the structural model of attitudes towards school subjects, academic aspiration and achievement and structural analysis revealed that 'attitudes to school' influence achievement, but only indirectly. Level of aspiration had significant direct effect on achievement and mediated between 'attitudes' and achievement.

Naglieri and Bornstein (2003) studied about self-concept and academic achievement in Slovenia and France and found that self-concept is significantly correlated with academic achievement.

Vaidya (2006) studied educational aspiration of higher secondary students and compare the academic achievement of students of formal and non-formal education and found that there was significant difference in the academic achievement between the students studying through formal and non-formal education in Telgu test; significant difference exist between students studying through formal and non-formal mode of education in their academic achievement in the areas of vocabulary, reading comprehension, writing and grammar; students from non-governmental school had higher educational aspiration than the students from government school.

Sharmistha (2008) has made a comparative study of factors affecting academic achievement of school going adolescent boys and girls and found that the factor like daily routine of the students tuitions' content viewed on TV were positively correlated with academic achievement and there is no significant gender difference seen in academic achievement.

Uniyal (2007) examined level of aspiration and scholastic achievement in relation to gender and caste with the objective to study the level of aspiration that determined the scholastic achievement by taking a sample of 514 adolescents and found that there exists a very high significant difference in between the high and low achiever students in overall aspiration scale; gender and achievement of students do have interactive effects on level of aspiration; level of aspiration was significantly influenced by scholastic achievement of students.

Tella, Tella, and Adeniy (2009) studied the locus of control, interest in schooling, self-efficacy and academic achievement and found that locus of control, interest in schooling and self-efficacy jointly and relatively contribute significantly to the prediction of academic achievement of the Junior Secondary School Students. Based on these findings, the need to continuously stimulate the interest of the students and teaching them time management and for teachers to see all the three variables on the study as important and improve them simultaneously was emphasized.

2. School Factors

The school determinants constitute probably the more recent research field on academic achievement. This concept to the effective school research, which has helped in the recognition of some variables and school operating patterns related with students performance as well as a more positive environment for learning. At the school level factors of academic achievement includes school environment, classroom environment, teaching methods, student teacher relationship etc. These factors along with some other factors are discussed below.

Classroom Environment

Classroom learning environment, referred to the classroom social atmosphere in which learning occurs. Fraser (1994) indicated these learning environments as the social-psychological contexts or determinants of learning.

Psychological environment refers to the social quality of the school and classroom; particularly it relates perceptions and feelings concerning social relationships among student and teachers (Arezoy, 2007). The classroom psychological environment, which refers to classroom social environment, classroom social interaction, and classroom social relationship are often used interchangeably when discussing the classroom learning environment (Cheng, 1994). Learning environment researches, which were firstly started in Western countries, showed strong emphasis on the use of a variety of validated questionnaires that assess student's perceptions of their classroom learning environment. Later, researches on learning environment were started in Asia countries and researchers have conducted studies that have cross-validated the main contemporary classroom environment questionnaires (e.g. Questionnaire on Teacher Interaction, Science Laboratory Environment Inventory, Constructivist Learning Environment Survey, and What Is Happening in This Class?) which were originally developed in English.

The classroom environment is the important determinant of student learning in educational system (Fraser, 1994, 1998a). Students learn better when they perceive their classroom environment more positively, hence the study of classroom environment has become a concern to educators, researchers, administrators of school system and parents. Numerous researches on classroom environment have been carried out years ago and have provided important information for educators and researchers on student's perception of classroom environment (Anderson & Walberg, 1974; Fraser, 1989; 1998a, 1998b; Nielson & Kirk, 1974).

Freiberg, (1998) stated that climate could positively influence the health of the learning environment, or it could significantly impede learning. Thus, feedback about climate could play an important role in reform. Masutha and Ackermann (1999), classroom climate significantly influences learner's achievement. A positive classroom climate that enhances academic achievement is facilitated by support, positive feedback, interest in learner's progress, and deliberation of learner's feelings.

Fraser and Fisher (1982) studied relationship between students affective and cognitive outcomes and their perceptions of classroom psychological environment as measured by the individualized classroom environment questionnaire (ICEQ) and the class room environment scale (CES) were investigated for a sample of 1,083 junior high school students in 116 classroom. Result showed that the ICEQ and CES give appreciable unique contribution to explaining outcomes variance.

Fraser (1984) studied the effects of classroom climate on student outcomes: A replication in two developing countries and found significant relationship between student outcomes and classroom climates among students in both Indonesia and Thailand.

Fraser (1986) studied differences between students and instructors perceptions of actual and preferred classroom environment and found that both students and instructors preferred a more favorable classroom environment than the one actually present and second instructors perceived the environment of their classes more positively than did their students in the same classrooms.

Schibeci (1987) studied effect of classroom environment on science attitudes, involved a total of 1125 secondary school students. This three phase study found statistically significant association between environment and attitudes.

Diekhoe, and Wigginton, (1992) studied college faculty perception of classroom environment and found that perceptions of classroom environment are linked to self-perceptions. The large college classroom appears to be sufficiently ambiguous that professors' perceptions of classroom environment reflect a self-projecting tendency.

Cheng (1994) studied about relationship between student affective performance and classroom physical environment, social climate and management style and found that good classroom environment is highly correlated with student affective performance.

Lim (1995) studied about perception of classroom environment, school types, Gender and learning styles of secondary school students. Two instrument the individual classroom environment questionnaire (ICEQ) and the learning style inventory 1985 (LSI) were administered in Singapore to a stratified random sample of 1733 secondary students from nine secondary schools, and found that school type had the most influence on the students perceptions of both actual and preferred classroom environment, gender had an influence too, but mainly on perceptions of actual classroom environment. Learning styles of students had the least influence.

Dorman (1997) studied the relationships between school and classroom environment. The study involved a sample of 2,211 students and found weak relationship between school and classroom environment.

Mc Robbie, Roth and Lucus, (1997) examined the multiple learning environment in a physics classroom and found that the nature of the classroom learning environment and psycho-social interaction can make a difference in how the students learn and achieve their goals

Hanrahan (1998) studied the effect of learning environment factors on students; Motivation and learning. This paper reports qualitative study of the learning environment of a year II biology class. The main method used for data gathering were participant observation, interviewing and a written response survey (CES, Tobin 1993) and found that even though the students viewed the class positively, and described themselves as highly motivated to learn, the level of cognitive engagement was affected by two interrelated factors, the control the hand over almost all activities, and student beliefs about learning in this context.

Backer (1999) studied the effect of teacher student interaction and relationship quality on student school /satisfaction in poor urban, African American Classrooms. He found that students who are dissatisfied with their classroom environment received less negative feedback when seeking assistance from their teacher and when teacher initiated contact regarding academic work but more negative feedback about their behavior when compared to students who were satisfied at school.

Kim (2000) studied classroom environment and teacher interpersonal behavior in Korea. The questionnaires were administered to 543 students in 12 different Korean schools and found positive relationships of classroom environment and interpersonal teacher behavior with students attitudinal outcome, Relative to girls, boys perceived their learning environments and their teachers interpersonal behavior more favorably and reported more favorable attitudes toward their science class.

Hopson (2001) studied the effect of a technology enriched classroom on student development of higher order thinking skills and student attitude towards computer. A sample of 80 sixth grade and 86 fifth grade students was tested using the Ross test of higher cognitive processes and surveyed using the computer attitude questionnaire. The creation of a technology enriched classroom environment appears to have had a positive effect on student acquisition of higher order thinking skills. This study identified several implications related to classroom design to enhance the development of higher order thinking skill. Teachers reported that the technology enriched classroom differed from the traditional classroom in several significant ways.

Ryan (2001) studied perception of the social environment of their eighth grade classroom related to change in motivation and engagement when they moved from seventh to eighth grade. In general, prior motivation and engagement whereas gender, race and prior achievement were not related to change in motivation or engagement.

Dorman, Fisher and Waldrip (2002) studied linking student's perception of learning environments and assessment with academic efficacy and attitude to science in Australian secondary schools. Result showed that classroom environment and student perceptions of assessment were significant positive predictors of academic efficacy and attitude to science.

Burnett (2002) studied the relationships between teacher praise and feedback, and students perceptions of the classroom environment. He found that negative teacher feedback and effort feedback were both related to students relationships with their teacher, while ability feedback was associated with perceptions of the classroom environment. Praise was not related to classroom environment or teacher student relationships.

Dorman, Adams, and Ferguson, (2003) studied association between classroom psychological environment in mathematics classroom and academic efficacy. A sample of 3,602 mathematics students from Australian, British and Canadian secondary schools responded to an instrument that assessed 10 dimensions of mathematics classroom environment (Vis. Student cohesiveness, teacher support, Investigation, task orientation, cooperation, equity, involvement, personal relevance, shared control, student negotiation) and found that classroom environment relates positively with academic efficacy.

A commonality analysis showed that the 3 constructivist learning environment survey scales did not contribute greatly to explaining variance in academic efficacy.

Beak and Choi (2002) studied relationship between students perceptions of classroom environment and their academic achievement in Korea and found that the seven subscales in the CES i.e. involvement, affiliation, and competition task orientation order and organization rule clarity and teacher control, had a significant correlation with students academic achievement.

Suzanna, (2003) studied classroom environment and academic performance at Kolei Yayasan Pelajaran Mara Kualalumpur and find out that student with good academic performance participated more actively in class compared to students with average and poor academic performance. Student who performed poorly in academic perceived the prevalence of teacher-student interaction in classroom but they were less confident to establish good rapport with their lectures. Good performance students regarded teachers' teaching efficiency highly, followed by the average and poor performing student respectively.

Sandra (2004) studied that how Teacher's beliefs about teaching and learning influence their instructional practices and students goals in the class room is important for understanding how to create learning environments focused on mastery and understanding, the current investigation examined relationships among teacher beliefs, instructional practices and classroom goal orientation in high school science classrooms. Path analysis techniques were used to analyze responses and revealed that personal teaching efficacy and teachers perceptions of a supporting school culture were related to teachers use of instructional practices focused on task master and understanding.

Chrisenduth (2006) studied influence of classroom climate on academic achievement of learners in secondary schools, and found that a significant positive correlation exists between classroom climate and academic achievement of learners in secondary schools. The research further confirmed that the lack of organization of learning space, lack of learner involvement in lessons and lack of classroom discipline contributes to poor academic achievement in secondary schools

Chang (2006) studied the possibilities of differential impact on students earth science learning outcomes between different actual learning environment spaces by using a newly developed ESCLEI (Earth science classroom learning environment instrument) and found that preferred actual space (PAS) between post treatment perception and pretreatment preferences accounted for a more substantial and statistically significant amount of learning outcomes in terms of students attitudes toward the subject matter with greater than large effect size, concerning practical significance in the actual earth science classroom. There finding suggest that earth science instruction in the secondary school should bridge the gap between students preferred / perceived learning environment with the aim to enhance their learning outcomes.

Talton and Simpson (2006) studied the relationship of classroom environment to attitudes towards science and achievement in science among tenth grade biology students the result of the study indicated that student attitudes towards the classroom environment predicted between 56 to 61% of the variance in attitudes towards science (2) student attitudes towards the classroom environment predicted between 5 to 14% of the variance in achievement in science. (3) Student attitudes towards science and attitudes toward the classroom environment predicted between 8 to 18% of the variance in achievement in science.

Wang and Thomas (2006) studied the effect of a web based learning environment on student motivation in a high school earth science course. The web LE was implemented in the teacher's tenth grade classroom as a three day student centered learning activity. This study revealed multiple forms of evidence that the web – LE and the associated learning activity improved students motivation.

Fraser (2007) studied classroom home and peer environment influence on student outcomes in science and mathematics. Finding confirmed the importance of extending research on classroom learning environment to include the learning environment of the home and the peer group. Only the classroom environment accounted for statistically significant amounts of unique variance in student achievement scores. Nazmiye Arisoy (2007) studied examining 874 grade students perception of learning environment of science classrooms in relation to motivational beliefs and attitudes and found that gender had a significant effect on students constructivist learning environment their adaptive motivational beliefs and their attitude towards science. He also found that all constructivist learning environment variables and all the motivational beliefs variables were positively related with each other.

Dorman (2008) studied students perceptions of actual and preferred classroom environment using, what is happening in the class? Questionnaire (WIHIC). A sample of 978 secondary school students from 63 classes in Queensland responded to the WIHIC and found statistically significant difference between actual and preferred environments and that the gap between actual and preferred environment was smaller for more positive classroom environments.

Furong (2008) studied the rural urban difference in classroom environment in compulsory education in the eastern coastal developed areas of China. He found that per capita GDP of a region is a main factor affecting classroom environment. The three main types of the actual classroom environment are high, middle and low ones, which distribute in a descending way in big cities, middle sized and countries and found significant difference between urban and rural areas.

Lau, and Lee (2008) studied Hong Kong students achievement goals and their relations with students perceived classroom environment and strategy use, based on the multiple goal perspective of goal orientation theory and find that students perceived classroom environment was significantly related to their personal achievement goals and strategy use.

Sungur, (2009) studied relationship between classroom environment perceptions self-regulation, and science achievement. He found that student's perception of classroom environment concerning motivating tasks autonomy support and mastery evaluation were positively associated with motivational and cognitive components of self-regulation and science achievement.

Guardino and Fullerton, (2010), examined changing behaviors by changing the classroom environment and stated that modifications to the classroom environment increased academic engagement and decreased disruptive behavior.

Okurut (2010) studied about secondary students, perception of mathematics classroom learning environment and their association with their motivation towards mathematics. A sample of 81 students (19 male 62 female) in two schools was used. Student perceptions of the classroom environment were assessed using a modified what is happening in this class? (WIHIC) questionnaire. The results suggest that teachers wishing to improve student motivation towards mathematics, in general, should emphasize the learning environment dimensions that are assessed by the WIHIC, the findings have implications for teachers of mathematics and head teachers particularly those in secondary schools.

Sadeghi (2010) studied about affecting the classroom psychological environment (CPE) on approaches of student learning in Guilan University, Iran. It focused on nine subscales of the CPE as involvement affiliation teacher support, task orientation, competition, order and organization, rule clarity teacher control and innovation. He found that the subscale of involvement had the largest discrepancy between preferred and actual form and the subscale of competition had the smallest discrepancy.

Okonkwo (2010) examined the relationship between secondary school students perceptions of classroom learning environment and their achievement in chemistry and found that high achievers among secondary school chemistry students had more positive perceptions of their classroom environment than the low achievers.

Okoh (2011) examined the comparison between perceptions of classroom environment by biology students in public and private secondary schools and found that high achievers in secondary school biology had more positive perception of their classroom environment than the low achievers.

Wei and Elias (2011) studied the relationship between students perception of classroom environment and their motivation in learning English language. The sample of study was 140 students in a secondary school in Malacca. The data were collected using questionnaires. The finding indicated that majority of the students perceived their classroom as having affiliation and they were extrinsically motivated. The finding also revealed that students, affiliation and task orientation in the classrooms were positive and significantly correlated with their motivation whereas students, involvement was negatively correlated.

Involvement

Measures the extent to which student have attentive interest in the class activities and participate in discussion and do additional work on their own and enjoy the class is considered.

Research evidence in the United States has suggested that student academic involvement is a powerful predictor of their achievement Wentzel (1993) Hong and Lee (2000) Rao and Moely and Sachs (2000) have shown that student academic engagement is positively related with their academic achievement.

According to Steyn (2001) learner involvement, support and encouragement are important factors influencing learner's success. Learner educator relationships are facilitated by co-operative, accepting environments whereas praise, recognition and respect contribute to creating positive classroom environment. Learner's achievement is enhanced when educators establish an academically demanding classroom that has clearly defined objectives, explicit instructions and an orderly and efficient environment. Astin's (1984) stated that "student involvement refers to the amount of physical and psychological energy that the student devotes to the academic experience." Astin describes an involved student is one who devotes energy to academics, spend a great deal of time on campus, participate in student organizations and activities and interacts with his or her faculty (Monroe Community College, 2004). Involvement theory states that students learn more when they are involved in all aspects of school life. An involved student will enjoy his or her experience and, in turn, stay in college (Huttey, 2004)

The consequence of student faculty interaction is critical; student involvement with faculty has a direct positive relationship to learning, academic performance and degree attainment (Astin, 1993). Students involvement in extracurricular activities is generally considered advantageous to their overall educational experience Interpersonal skills and leadership abilities increased with student involvement. Student satisfaction also improved with student involvement in student life functions (Astin, 2001). Evidence suggests that participating in extracurricular activities integrates students and has a positive impact for "persistence and degree competition" (Pascarella & Terenzini, 1991). He told (1991) that students who interact with faculty, staff, and their peers outside of the classroom form educated opinions, attitudes, values, and aspirations based on those interactions. Students create their identity and become autonomous when they become engaged and involved in out of class activities. House, (2000) studied the effects of student involvement on the development of academic self-concept and found that involvement in campus activity increase confidence and leadership skill.

Learning communities are another place where students can become involved on campus learning enhanced when interaction between new students and their poor, faculty and staff increases (Banta, 2001). Northern Arizona University (NAU) revealed that involvement equals retention (Nason-Saltonstall, 2004). Students who feel connected to their college campus appear to feel better about their experience and, in turn, stay through graduation (Astin, 2001; Kentuky Council on Post-secondary Education, 2007). Garland (2010) studied "Assessing the relationship between student involvement and academic performance in higher education and found significant relationships between GPA and the number of student organizations in which they participated, officer status within student organizations, and the length of time of participation in student organization(s).

Affiliation

Affiliation assess the level of friendship students feel for each other i.e. the extent to which they help each other with homework get to know each other easily, and enjoy working together. Students relationships within classroom were related to students academic progress. Adolescents spend a large amount of time with their peers during the course of each school day it is rational to expect that they influence one another's academic engagement and achievement outcomes. Researcher revealed that peers affect all facts of a student's life, mainly social and emotional adjustment, educational aspirations and day to day behavior in school (e.g. Berndt, 1999; Fuligni *et al.*, 2001; Steinberg, Dornbusch and Brown, 1992). Fuligni *et. al.,* 2001 found peer influence peaks during adolescence. Lubbers, (2006) studied the impact of peer relations on academic progress in junior high school and found that students who were accepted by their peers had lower probabilities to retain a grade or to move downward in the tract system.

Jacobson and Burdral (2012) studied academic performance in middle school: Friendship influences Result support that adolescents' relationships with peers influence academic performance specifically social support was significantly and positively related to academic performance.

Teacher Support

Measures the amount of help, concern and friendship the teacher directs toward the students. Teacher plays a vital role to create environment that supports effective teaching and learning in the classrooms. Thus the organization of learning space: learner involvement and discipline in the classroom are important factors influencing academic achievement. Teacher support refers to students beliefs that their teachers care about them, value them and establish personal relationships with them (e.g., Fraser & Fisher, 1982; Goodenow, 1993; Trickett & Moos, 1973). Researchers have found positive associations between perceptions of teacher support and students adaptive motivational beliefs and engagement behaviors. when students view their teacher as supportive they report higher levels of interest, valuing, effort, and enjoyment in their school work (Fraser & Fisher, 1982; Midgley, Feldlafer & Eccles,1989; Trickett & Moos, 1974), a more positive academic self-concept (Felner, Aber, Primavera, & Cauce, 1985), and greater expectancies for success (Goodenow, 1993). Perceiving the teacher as supportive is also related positively to asking for help with school work when needed (Newman & Schwager, 1993), use of self-regulated learning strategies (Ryan & Patrick, 2001), and a desire to comply with classroom rules (Wentzel, 1994). Perceived teacher support is related negatively to absenteeism (Moos & Moos, 1978) and disruptiveness in the classroom (Ryan & Patrick, 2001).

Bartholomyh (1996) studied "student and teachers as partners in the classroom community: A study of classroom social environment and found that significant difference in students perceptions of the ideal and actual classroom social environment". Students indicated a preference for significantly more involvement, affiliation teacher support, personal goal attainment, organization and clarity and student influence than they saw in their actual classroom environment. Students preferred ideal classroom environments in which they could be actively involved in the learning process. They indicated a preference for interactional activities with other students and with their instructors. Students expressed interest in opportunities for exploring personal interest in relation to the course, relating their courses to their own experiences and having opportunities to be partners with the teacher in planning for class activities to support the concepts of the course.

Goh and Khine (2002) found that a good teacher-student relationship is superior to the formation and maintenance of a positive classroom environment. Ma, (2003) studied the "Sense of belonging to school: Can school make a difference?" and stated that Student perception of teacher support have been related with greater feelings of school belonging and greater school engagement and motivation as well as better academic performance.

Montalve, Mansfield and Miller (2007) studied the liking or disliking the teacher: Student motivation, engagement and achievement and found that students will put forth greater effort and demonstrate a higher degree of persistence if they like their teachers. Finding also indicates that students attain better grades in classes taught by teachers they like. Teachers liked by students shared characteristics such as constructing a classroom setting with an emphasis on learning, giving effective feedback, and encouraging tenacity when work becomes challenging these traits all increase student achievement.

Hallinan (2008) studied the teacher influences on students attachment to school and found that when students needs to be valued and respected are met, their attachment to school increases.

Ushakumari (2008) studied the relationship of teacher aptitude with academic achievement and certain psychological variables of primary teacher. Trainees of Kerala and found aptitude towards teaching profession as the major variable having relation. Significant relationship with teacher aptitude and its entire four constructs viz., instructional awareness, educational problem solving, creativity and mental ability.

Chiaki Konishi (2010) examine "Do school bullying and Student–Teacher relationships matter for academic achievement" and found that positive teacher-student relationship were associated with better school performance.

Task Orientation/Competition/Teacher Control

Research suggested that student academic engagement is a significant predictor of their academic achievement (Wentzel, 1993). Students academic engagement is positively associated with their achievement outcomes (Hong & Lee, 2000; Rao, Moely, and Sachs, 2000). Hong and Lee found that high achieving group were more self-motivated, persistent and responsible in doing their homework than low achieving group.

Gneezy, Niederle and Rustichini (2003) studied performance in competitive environments: gender differences and found that, as we increase the competitiveness of the environment, a significant increase in performance for men, but not for women. This result shows significant gender gap in performance.

Lam, Yim, Law, and Cheung (2004) studied the effects of competition on achievement motivation in Chinese classrooms and found that competition had a positive impact on performance goals and learning motivation in the classroom.

Classroom control has often been defined as a single dimension running from teacher control to student autonomy. Classroom discipline that promotes academic achievement reflects learner behavior that is not disorderly and does not interfere with the activities of the lesson. Classroom management strategies indicate that educators act according to code of conduct of the school when learners break rules they try to understand learners behavior and provide support. Learners in orderly classrooms are extrinsically motivated when educators provide positive feedback and frequent verbal support and praise four distinct perceived classroom control styles were determined, based on the balance between teacher and student control over learning.

Eshel and Kohavi (2003) studied on perceived classroom control, self-regulated learning strategies, and academic achievement and found significant relationship between four classroom control style and student achievement.

Dettmer (2004) posited that "learning by losing" was a valuable process for students preparing for professions where working under pressure was necessary.

Kiany and Shayestefar, (2011) studied high school students perceptions of EFL teacher control orientations and their English academic achievement. Sample consist of 732 English (EFL English as a Foreign language) students studying in three major field of high school (Mathematics Natural Science and Humanities). The result of multilevel analysis explained that relatively large amount of variance was found by the control variable and student variable and teacher control had a statistically significant effect on student outcomes many factors within classrooms can effect students' academic performance. In particular, the authority structure of classrooms that encourages students to be autonomous in their learning is related to their intrinsic motivation. Similarly, one important factor linked to classroom climate is teachers' control orientation. Teachers' orientations whether they believe that children should be controlled or be given freedom to make decision determines the structure of classrooms which in turn effect students motive to learn (Deci, Schwartz, Shenman & Ryan, 1981). Cornell and Welborn (1991) and Ryan and Powelson's (1991) model suggesting that in the classroom the autonomy support and caring or relatedness are intertwined and satisfy students needs for autonomy and belonging which are necessary for optimal learning environment.

Akhtar (2003) examined the relationships between teachers' control orientations, perceived teachers' control behavior and students motivation and he found that caring and humanistic classroom climate enhances students social motivation, social motivation and their relation with teachers and peers, strongly influence their academic performance.

Innovation

Woodward and Baxter (1997) studied the effects of innovative approach to mathematics on academically low achieving students in mainstreamed setting and found that Innovative methods in Mathematics are viable for students with average and above average academic abilities and that students with learning disabilities or those at risk for special education need much greater assistance if they are to be included in general education classrooms. The extent to which the teacher attempts to use new techniques and attempts to use new techniques and encourages creative thinking in the students in considered.

Wong, Li, Choi and Lee (2008) studied "Insights into Innovative Classroom Practices with ICT: Identifying the Impetus for Chang" and found that ICT has made a positive impact on changing the modes of teaching and learning in classroom practices from a teacher centered approach to one that is student centered, irrespective of region, school level and type of school.

SOCIO-CULTURAL FACTORS

Sex

Refers to a person's biological status and is typically categorized as male, female, or intersex (i.e., typical combinations of features that usually distinguish male from female) and gender refers to the attitudes, feelings, and behaviors that a given culture associates with a person's biological sex. Over the last decade there has been evidence of a growing gender gap in academic achievement (Fergusson & Horwood, 1997; Hillman & Rothman, 2003; Praat, 1999; Thiessen & Nickerson,1999; Weaver-Hightower, 2003). Educational statistics have indicated that females are outperforming males at all levels of the school system, attaining more school and post-school qualifications, and attending university in higher numbers (Alton Lee & Praat 2001; House of Representatives Standing Committee on Education and Training, 2002; Mullis *et. al.,* 2003; Office for Standards in Education, 2003). Although males have traditionally out performed females in mathematics and science, this advantage now disappearing (Benbow & Stanley, 1980; Hyde, Fennema & Lamon, 1990; Hyde & Linn, 2006; Spelke, 2005). These findings have caused widespread concern about male educational achievement and have led to considerable speculation and discussion about the origins of gender differences in education.

Several studies have provided reports that there are no longer distinguishing differences in the cognitive, affective and psychomotor skill achievements of students in respect of gender (Arigbabu & Mji 2004; Bilesanmi-Awoderu, 2006; David & Stanley, 2000; Din, Ming, & Esther, 2004; Freedman, 2002; Sungur & Tekkaya, 2003, etc.). However, Aguele and Uhumniah (2008); Billings (2000); Croxford (2002); Eccles, Lord, Roeser, Barber, and Jozefowicz (1997); Hyde and McKinley, (1997); Kolawole, (2007), etc., in their studies found that male students performed better than female students in the cognitive, affective and psychomotor skill achievements. Studies conducted by Billings, (2000), Eccles, Lord, Roeser, Barber, and Jozefowwicz (1997) Aguele and Uhumniah (2008) found, that male students achieved significantly better than female students in science education.

Samuel and John (2004) examined how the cooperative class experiment (CCE) teaching methods affect students achievement in Chemistry. They found that there was no significant difference in gender achievement between the experimental and control groups, but girls had a slightly higher mean score than boys did.

Kolawole (2007) found that boys performed better than girls in both cooperative and competitive learning strategies when he conducted a research on the effects of competitive and cooperative learning strategies on Nigerian students' academic performance in mathematics.

Oludipe (2012) studied gender difference in Nigerian junior secondary students academic achievement in basic science and found there was no significant difference in academic achievement of male and female students at the pretest, posttest, and delayed posttest levels respectively. Findings of this research recommended that in order to encourage more women into pure sciences, and science-oriented courses, interventions need to be designed that focus not only on the academic achievement of girls but also in how to make science-related occupations more interesting for young, high achieving girls.

Parental Education

Many factors influence a child's academic achievement beyond a child's innate ability, the neighborhoods children live in, the qualities of the school and parents education, Income of the family etc. all have an effect. According to the National Institute of Health, the education level of a parent is a significant predictor of a child's educational achievements and behavior outcomes.

Possibly the most important and direct explanation of the link between parent's education and their children's academic achievement relies on the assumption that parents learn something during schooling that influence the way in which they interact with their children around learning activities in the home (Crowny & Bradley 2002; Pamela & Kean 2005)

The Literature on achievement constantly has shown that parent education is important in predicting children's achievement (Klebanav, Brooks – Gunn & Dunkan, 1994; Haveman & Wolfe, 1995; Smith, Brooks – Gunn & Klebandv, 1997). Majority of the literature on parents, education pertains to the direct, position influence on achievement (Jimerson, Egeland & Teo, 1999; Luster Rhoades & Haas, 1989). The literature also suggests that it influences the beliefs and behaviors of the parent, leading the positive outcomes for children and youth (Eccles, 1993); Klebanov, Brooks – Gunn and Dunkan (1994) found that both mother's education and family income were important predictors of the physical environment and learning experience in the home bat that mothers' education alone was predict of parental warmth. Smith Brooks Gunn and Klebandv (1997) found that the association of family income and parents education with children's academic achievement was mediated by the home environment, if the parents are educated, the more elevated is the socio-economic status and more satisfaction stems from it, along with concomitant privileges, facilities and behavioral stances (Khan, Anila & Pervez 1991. There is considerable evidence pointing to the level of parental education as a strong predictor of children's success in the educational system Crowyn and Bradley (2002) also found that maternal education has the most consistent direct influence on children's cognitive and behavioral outcomes.

Socioeconomic Status (SES)

Socioeconomic status (SES) is evaluated as a grouping of factors including income, level of education, and occupation. It is a way of looking at how persons or families fit into society using economic and social measures that have been shown to impact individuals' health and well-being. Socioeconomic status and health are closely related, and SES can often have profound effects on a person's health due to differences in ability to access health care as well as dietary and other life style choices that are associated with both finances and education.

Significant studies have suggested that socioeconomic status is one of the best predictors of student achievement (Coleman, *et. al.,* 1966; Lee, Bryk, & Smith, 1993). Parents educational status is considered one of the most stable aspects of Socio Economic Status (SES) because it is typically established at an early age and tends to remain the same over time (Sirin, 2005). It has been well documented that family plays a meaningful role in a child's academic performance and development (Cornell & Grossberg, 1987; Thompson, Alexander, & Entwisle, 1988; Tucker, Harris, Brady, & Herman, 1996). Mothers' levels of education and family incomes influence adolescent educational outcome expectancy beliefs (Rhea & Otto, 2001). A study by Campbell, Hombo and Mazzeo (1999) using NAEP data indicated that students who reported higher parental education levels tended to have higher average scores. Many factors in the family background have some associations with students success throughout school and in young adults' eventual educational and occupational attainment. Such variables include family structure (socioeconomic status and intact/single parent families), parental education level, parental involvement and parenting style (Jacob & Harvey, 2005). More educated parents are assumed to create environments that facilitate learning (Williams, 1980; Teachman, 1987) and involve themselves in their children school experiences and school environments (Steinberg *et. al.*, 1992; Useem, 1992). However, there are students who come from low-income and single parent homes who are high achievers and many students from high socio-economic and intact families who are low achievers. Students may also come from homes where the parents are highly educated and involved in their children's education, yet achieve poorly at school (Jacob and Harvey, 2005).

Casanova, *et. al.,* (2005) studied on influence of family and socio demographic variables on students with low academic achievement and found differential pattern in the prediction of academic success. In the group of adolescents with normal academic achievement, socio-demographic variables better predict achievement, for students with low achievement, family variable play a more important role in predicting achievement.

Farooq, Chaudhury, Shafiq and Berhanu (2011) studied factors affecting students quality of academic performance and found that SES and parents education have a significant effect on students over all academic achievement. The high and average socio-economic level affects the performance more than the lower level. It is very interesting that parents academic performance more than their occupation in relation to their children's academic performance at school.

Gupta, Sharma and Gupta (2012) studied the gender difference on the measure of academic achievement in adolescent students and found no significant difference between boys and girls.

Suleman *et. al.,* (2012) studied the effect of parental socio-economic status on the academic achievement of secondary school students and found that parental SES, parents educational level, parental occupational level; and parental income level effect the academic achievement of students at secondary level. Therefore, it is strongly recommended that unemployment should be controlled and poor students should be provided scholarship, free books and other stationary.

Ogunshola and Adewale (2012) studied the effect of parental socio-economic status on academic performance of students in selected schools in Edu Lga of Kwara State Nigeria and found that parental educational qualification and health statuses of the students were identified statistical significant effect to the academic performance of the students. Hence, home environment played notable role in the academic achievement of the respondents. However, parental SES and parental education background did not have significant effect on the academic performance of the students.

Locale

Locale is a demographic variable consider under the category of social variable in this study. People inhabit different parts of the world and lead different types of lives, their lifestyle change across the various region of this world and so do their thought processes. People all over the world have been divided into two distinct group is, classified as rural or urban depending on the density of human created structure and resident people in a particular area. The resources found in their regions or areas have a direct impact on their way of living.

Boylan and Mcswan (1978) reported that rural school were inferior and lacking in the range of facilities with high staff turnover and suffered from lack of continuity in their curriculum. Obe (1984) observed a significant difference in rural-urban academic performance on the aptitude sub tests of the National Common Entrance Examination in to Secondary Schools. He concluded that children from urban schools were superior to their rural counterparts. Some of the researchers namely, Edington and Martellaro (1984), Ward and Murray (1985) found no significant differences in the outcomes of students at urban and rural schools.

Blackwell and McLaughlin (1999), find the rural-urban location variable to be significant in explaining performance. The debate on the impact of this variable centers on the possibility that the differences in the performance of students in rural and urban schools are not due to the location per se, but rather to the fact that the characteristics of the students, their families and the schools differ in these two groups. Students in rural zones typically belong to families with few financial resources, their parents have low levels of education and the schools they attend are usually poorly endowed in terms of facilities and they are, generally, smaller than urban schools.

Fan and Chen (1999) studied academic achievement of rural school students: A multi-year comparison with their peers in sub-urban and urban schools and found that, all else equal, rural students do not suffer disadvantage simply as the result of their residence in rural areas or their attendance at rural schools. Roscigno and Crowley (2001) reported that the academic performance of rural children typically lags behind that of urban children. Howley (2002) reported that there is no difference between rural and urban education. Owoeye (2002) found that there was a significant difference between academic performance of students in rural and urban area in public examinations. Nagaraju, Sumalatha, and Reddy, (2003) reported that the achievement of the pupils from urban areas was better than the achievement of pupils from rural areas.

Singh and Singh (2007) studied the impact of caste, gender and habitat on achievement in Mathematics at upper primary school level with the objective to study the impact of caste, gender and habitat on achievement by taking a sample of 200 students of eighth class and found that boys were better than girls on achievement in Mathematics and students of urban areas were better in achievement than the students of rural areas.

Usha (2007) revealed that urban pupils were found superior to rural pupils in their achievement. Bamman and. Ksheersagar (2008) found that achievement of the pupils from urban areas were better than the achievement of pupils from rural areas.

Dhanda and Singh (2009) found that urban area surpassed children from rural area in intelligence. Elizabeth (2009) found significant difference in academic achievement of the student, She found rural students have higher academic achievement than urban students. Joshi and Srivastava (2009) reported that the achievement of the pupils from urban areas was better than the achievement of pupils from rural areas.

Wobmann (2010), reported no significant differences in the outcomes of students attending rural and urban schools in Argentina.

Sing (2012) studied academic achievement of IXth class students of district Solan of Himachal Pradesh in relation to their area of residence and self-concept and found no significant difference in the academic achievement of students at different levels of their self-concept.

Alokan *et. al.,* (2013) studied about rural and urban differential in student's academic performance among secondary school students in Ondo State, Nigeria and his study revealed that there is no significant difference in the academic performance of students from rural environment. It can be concluded from the result that, all else equal, rural students do not suffer disadvantage in their academic performance simply as the result of their residence in rural areas or their attendance at rural schools. It was recommended; among others that rural deficit model should be further examined as educators take a new and more objective look at the performance of the many different types of rural students. Also, parents and students should not feel that they must attend metropolitan schools in order to achieve success.

3

Problems and Hypotheses

The present chapter deals with the formulation of objectives and hypotheses of research study undertaken. As a nation, we are focused on raising the level of academic achievement in our schools. The learning climate that is determined by the organization of learning space learner involvement in lessons and discipline in the classroom are often unnoticed in the assessment process. However these variables significantly influence academic achievement of students. The literature review clearly indicates that there is a greater need for emphasis on the classroom climate that may enhance academic achievement of students, the learning environment has a big influence on student outcomes and plays an important role in improving the effectiveness of learning in all levels of classrooms. Studies consistently have shown evidence of relations between student perceptions of their classroom learning environment and their outcomes (Chionh & Fraser, 1998; Fraser & Fisher, 1982; Fraser, 1986, 1989, 1994; Haertel, Walberg, & Haertel, 1981; Henderson, Fisher & Fraser, 2000; Hunus & Fraser, 1997; Koul & Fisher, 2002; Margianti, Fraser & Aldridge, 2001; Myint & Goh, 2001; Roth, 1998). Students learn better when they perceive their classroom environment positively (Chionh & Fraser, 1998). Positive school environment is recognized as a significant component of thriving and effective schools (Brand, Felner, Shim, Seitsinger & Dumas,

2003; Miller & Fredericks, 1990). It is defined as shared beliefs, values, and attitudes that shape relations between students, teachers, and administrators and place the parameters of adequate behavior and norms for the school (Emmons, Comer, & Haynes, 1996; Kuperminc, Leadbeater, Emmons, & Blatt, 1997). School climate is a product of social relations among students and with teachers, is influenced by educational and social values, and has been shown to relate to social situations within classrooms and to the school as a whole. It has been linked to academic achievement (Battistich, Solomon, Kim, Watson, & Schaps, 1995; Griffith, 1999); student misconduct, aggression, and behavioral problems (Battistich & Hom, 1997; Battistich, Solomon, Kim, Watson, & Schaps, 1995; Shochet, Dadds, Ham, & Montague, 2006; Welsh, 2000; Wilson, 2004); adjustment problems (Kuperminc *et. al.,* 1997); and social and personal attitudes (Battistich *et. al.,* 1995). Although these studies revealed that academic achievement has been debated and researched extensively. The review of literature reveals that academic achievement has been studied by a number of researches but it does not seem to be studied in connection with classroom environment in rural and urban perspective in Chhattisgarh region. There is need of more studies and researches to find out the relationship between perceived classroom environment of the rural and urban students and their academic achievement. Therefore, The present study has been undertaken with a view to investigate the relationship of perceived classroom environment along with its various sub dimensions namely involvement, affiliation, teacher support, task orientation, competition, order organization, rule clarity, teacher control and innovation, locale and sex with academic achievement of the students.

Classroom Environment and Academic Achievement

Studies have shown evidence of relations between classroom learning environment and their outcomes (Fraser & Aldridge, 2001; Fraser & Fisher, 1982; Fraser,1994; Hunus & Fraser, 1997; Koul & Fisher, 2002; Myint & Goh, 2001). Students learn better when they perceive their classroom environment positively (Chinon & Fraser, 1998). Learning is an active, process, it presupposes active involvement by the learner in the act of learning before it can take place. As a result of active involvement learners learn what they are expected to learn to their fullest potential. In a positive classroom climate learners are happy and a enjoy going to school, and educators work together in a systematic way to achieve their objectives (Chrispeels, 1992). Research evidence in the united states has suggested that student academic involvement is a powerful predictor of their achievement Wentzel 1993; Hong and Lee (2000), Rao & Moely and Sachs (2000) have shown that student academic engagement is positively associated with their achievement.

(Berndt, 1999; Fuligni *et. al.*, 2001; Steinberg, Dornbusch & Brown, 1992) revealed that peers affect all facts of a student's life, especially social and emotional adjustment, educational aspirations and day to day behavior in school and peer influence peaks during adolescence.

Student perception of teacher support have been associated with greater feelings of school belonging (Ma, 2003 & Osterman, 2000) and greater school engagement and motivation as well as better academic performance (Birch & Ladd, 1998) positive teacher-student relationship were associated with better school performance (Chiaki Konishi, 2010).

Teacher support in the classroom have been consistently linked with increased student achievement motivation and academic success, students relationships with teacher become increasingly significant as they look for role models and support. Research shows that student who feel that educators encourage them are more committed to learning and are more successful academically. The impact of classroom climate on students and staff can be beneficial for or a barrier to learning,

Researchers have found positive associations between perceptions of teacher support and students adaptive motivational beliefs and engagement behaviors. When students view their teacher as supportive they report higher levels of interest, valuing, effort, and enjoyment in their school work (Fraser & Fisher, 1982; Midgley *et. al.,* 1989; Trickett & Moos, 1974), a more positive academic self-concept (Felner, Aber, Primavera, & Cauce, 1985), and greater expectancies for success (Goodenow, 1993). Perceiving the teacher as supportive is also related positively to asking for help with school work when needed (Newman & Schwager, 1993), use of self-regulated learning strategies (Ryan & Patrick, 2001), and a desire to comply with classroom rules (Wentzel, 1994). Perceived teacher support is related negatively to absenteeism (Moos & Moos, 1978) and disruptiveness in the classroom (Ryan & Patrick, 2001). Research suggested that student academic engagement is a significant predictor of their academic achievement (Wentzel, 1993). Students academic engagement is positively associated with their achievement outcomes (Hong & Lee, 2000; Rao, Moely, and Sachs, 2000).

Taking these facts into consideration present study would test the hypothesis that classroom environment along with its various sub dimensions would show significant role in determining the academic achievement. It is hypothesized that classroom environment (along with its dimensions i. e. involvement, affiliation teacher support, task orientation, competition, order organization, rule clarity, teacher control and innovation) would contribute significantly to academic achievement of the student.

Locale and Academic Achievement

The next problem of the study is to investigate the role of locale in academic achievement in relation to various dimensions of classroom environment. The word locale refers to the residential background of the individuals. Here two types of locale, i. e., rural and urban were considered for study. Boylan and Mcswan (1978) reported that rural school were inferior and lacking in the range of facilities with high staff turnover and suffered from lack of continuity in their curriculum. Obe (1984) observed a significant difference in rural-urban academic performance. He concluded that children from urban schools were superior to their rural counterparts. Blackwell and McLaughlin (1999), found the rural-urban location variable to be significant in explaining performance. Owoeye (2002) found that there was a significant difference between academic performance of students in rural and urban area in public examinations. Nagaraju *et. al.*, (2003) reported that the achievement of the pupils from urban areas was better than the achievement of pupils from rural areas. Usha (2007) revealed that urban pupils were found superior to rural pupils in their achievement. Bamman and Ksheersagar (2008) found that achievement of the pupils from urban areas were better than the achievement of pupils from rural areas. Dhanda and Singh (2009) found that urban area surpassed children from rural area in intelligence. Joshi and Srivastava (2009) reported that the achievement of the pupils from urban areas was better than the achievement of pupils from rural areas.

Taking these facts into consideration present study would test the hypothesis that locale would show significant role in determining the academic achievement. It is hypothesized that locale would predict significantly to academic achievement of the student in relation to various dimensions of classroom environment namely, involvement, affiliation teacher support, task orientation, competition, order organization, rule clarity, teacher control and innovation.

SEX AND ACADEMIC ACHIEVEMENT

The last problem of the study is to investigate the role of sex in academic achievement in relation to various dimensions of classroom environment. Over the last decade there has been evidence of a growing gender gap in educational achievement. Fergusson & Horwood, 1997; Hillman & Rothman, 2003; Praat, 1999; Thiessen & Nickerson, 1999; Weaver-Hightower, 2003. Educational statistics have indicated that females are outperforming males at all levels of the school system, attaining more school and post-school qualifications, and attending university in higher numbers (Alton Lee & Praat 2001; House of Representatives Standing Committee on Education and Training, 2002; Mullis *et. al.,* 2003; Office for Standards in Education, 2003). Research on gender differences in classroom environment perceptions was also conducted in various countries (Fisher, Fraser & Rickards, 1997; Fisher, Rickards, Goh, & Wong, 1997; Fraser, Giddings & Mc Robbie, 1995; Henderson, Fisher & Fraser, 2000; Wong & Fraser, 1997). Owens and Straton (1980) found that girls preferred cooperation more than boys but boys preferred competition and individualization more than girls. Overall, these studies have shown that girls generally hold more favorable perceptions of their classroom learning environments than boys in the same classes.

Taking these facts into consideration present study would test the hypothesis that sex would show significant role in determining the academic achievement. It is hypothesized that sex would predict significantly to academic achievement of the student in relation to various dimensions of classroom environment.

4

Method

In this chapter attempt has been made to discuss the sample, the measures used, the design and the procedure of data collection. In the design section, the type of design and the statistics used to explain the relationship of dependent variable academic achievement with independent variables (classroom environment, locale and sex) has been discussed.

SAMPLE

Initially a larger number of students studying in class X of different state government higher secondary schools of Chhattisgarh state were randomly selected, out of which 947 subjects were retained as final sample. In the present study the sample were selected from two different locales i.e. rural and urban. The age range of the subjects was 15-17 years. Details of the sample are mentioned in Table 1.

Table 1. Details of the sample used in the present study. Figures in each cell indicate the number of subjects used

	Rural	*Urban*	*Total*
Male	266	185	451
Female	292	204	496
Total	558	389	947

MEASURES

To assess classroom environment, Classroom Environment Scale (CES) constructed and standardized by Moos and Trickett

(1974), adaptation and standardization to suit the Indian conditions in Hindi Joshi and Vyas (1987) is used. CES scale has four dimensions comprising of nine subscales which reflect a conceptualization of the relationships among them. The four dimensions and the nine sub-dimensions are as follows:

The four dimensions and the nine sub-dimension are as follows:

Table 2.
Classroom environment dimension and sub dimension

No	Dimensions	Sub-dimensions
1.	*Relationship* – measures the extent to which students have attentive interest in class activities and participated in discussion do additional work on their own and enjoy the class is considered. The nature and intensity of personal relationship within the environment and the extent to which people are involved in the environment and support one another – *involvement, affiliation, teacher support*	*Involvement* – measures the extent to which student have attentive interest in the class activities and participate in discussion. The extent to which students do additional work on their own and enjoy the class is considered. *Affiliation* – assesses the level of friendship student feel for each other i.e.., the extent to which they help each other with homework, get to know each other easily and working together. *Teacher support* – measures the amount of help, concern and friendship the teacher directs toward the students.
2.	*Personal Development* –The basic direction along which personal growth and self-enhancement tend to occur – *task orientation, competition*	*Task orientation* measure the extent to which it is important to complete the activities that have been planned. *Competition* assesses the emphasis placed on student competing with each other for grades recognition.

3.	*System Maintenance* – the extent, to which the environment is orderly, clear in expectation, maintains control and is responsive to change – *order and organization, rule clarity, teacher control.*	*Order and organization* assess the emphasis on students behaving in an orderly and polite manner and on the overall organization of assignment and classroom activity. *Rule clarity* assess the emphasis on establishing and following a clear set of ruler and on student knowing what the extent to which teacher with student who break ruler. *Teacher control* – measure how strict the teacher is in enforcing the ruler and the severity of the punishment for rules infraction.
4.	*System Change* – It include innovation which measures how much student contributes to planning classroom activities and the amount of unusual and varying activities and assignment planned by the teacher. The extent to which the teacher attempts to use new technique and encourage creative thinking in the students is considered.	*Innovation* – measure how much student contributes to planning classroom activities and the amount of unusual and varying activities and assignment planned by teacher.

Classroom environment scale consist of 78 items which cover the almost all the important constitutes of its main dimension, i.e. Involvement, Affiliation, Teacher Support, Task Orientation, Competition, Order and Organization, Rule Clarity, Teacher Control and Innovation.

To assess academic achievement of the student, overall marks obtained by the student in different subjects, viz- Hindi, English, Mathematics, Science, and Social Science in class 10th board examination was used.

DESIGN

The present study is a co-relational research employing type-S independent variables. The main objective of the study is to find out the relationship of academic achievement with classroom environment along with its dimensions, locale and sex. The predictors undertaken in the study are perceived classroom environment along with its nine dimensions (i.e. involvement, affiliation, teacher support, task orientation, competition, order and organization, rule clarity, teacher control and innovation), locale and sex. The criterion variable is academic achievement of the student. To fulfill the above mentioned objective Pearson s' product moment coefficient of correlation and multiple regression analysis technique is applied. The variables under taken in the present study are:

Criterion Variable – Academic Achievement

Predictors:

A. Classroom environment
B. Locale
C. Sex

A. Classroom environment:

1. Involvement
2. Affiliation
3. Teacher support
4. Task orientation
5. Competition
6. Order and organization
7. Rule clarity
8. Teacher control
9. Innovation

B. Locale:

1. Urban
2. Rural

C. Sex:

1. Male
2. Female

Procedure

After explaining the objectives of the research work permission was obtained from the principles of the selected schools. To administer the questionnaires to the students of tenth standard. To establish a good rapport with the subject it was assured that their responses and identities would be strictly kept confidential and not disclose anywhere. Thus they were made independent to give their answer comfortably and honestly, whatever they felt. In this way subjects were encouraged to give their proper cooperation during the testing.

The classroom environment scale booklets were distributed to the subjects. The printed instructions were explained to the subjects. The subjects were seated in group settings. A response sheet was provided with each booklet for the subjects to mark their responses. The classroom were the test was conducted was well organized and the seating arrangement was also made comfortable. After the completion of test booklets were also collected back. The participant students, principal and the staffs of the school were given thanks for their cooperation.

After having administered the test as per procedure laid down and collection of the answer sheets and booklets is to be completed. The scoring of the data was done as per the norms of scoring. Responses of the respondents in the form of raw scores are given in appendix-B.

It must be noted that each item of every scale is on a five point scale of "4 to Zero" There are some negatively framed items for which the scoring is in reverse direction of scoring weightage, i.e. "zero to 4".

The total score of each sub scale has to be obtained by adding score obtained on each respective items of that scale. Thus, for each sub scale total score is obtained and interpreted.

After scoring, the data was organized and put for the statistical analysis. The data was analyzed with the help of appropriate statistical techniques, in order to verify the formulated hypotheses the results and discussion are presented in the next chapter.

A copy of scale is enclosed in Appendix A. Academic achievement scores of the respondents in the form of raw scores are given in Appendix B.

5

Results and Discussion

The purpose of the present study was to examine the role of classroom environment along with its various dimensions, locale and sex on academic achievement of the student. To realize the main objective the sample for the present study was taken from government schools of Chhattisgarh State. The obtained data were analyzed by applying coefficient of correlation, stepwise multiple regression analysis technique using the statistical package for social science (SPSS) 16th version. In the present study independent variables are classroom environment with its nine sub dimensions namely involvement, affiliation, teacher support, task orientation, competition, order and organization, rule clarity, teacher control and innovation, locale and sex and the academic achievement (i.e. overall marks obtained by the student and subject wise marks) comprised as the dependent variable. Among independent variables locale and sex were in categories, but for the purpose of the present analysis they were treated as dummy variables and scoring has been done accordingly as below:

Variables	**Scoring**	**Dummy Name**
Locale	Urban-1	Ruralness
	Rural-2	
Sex	Male-1	Femininity
	Female-2	

After dummy variable scoring, they have been considered as metric variables and scores were treated as on rating scales. Stepwise multiple regression analysis technique was employed to examine the role of independent variables to determine dependent variable. The problem and hypotheses undertaken for the present study and obtained results are discussed in the light of existing literature are as under:

RESULTS OF DESCRIPTIVE STATISTICS REGARDING ACADEMIC ACHIEVEMENT

Mean value and S.D. obtained on overall marks (academic achievement) for rural, urban, male female and for total are shown in table 3 and fig. 1.

Table 3. Average academic achievement scores for urban, rural, male, female and for total

Variable	Mean	S.D.
Urban	229.02	66.05
Rural	244.57	63.91
Male	238.97	70.84
Female	237.41	59.0
Total	238.15	65.18

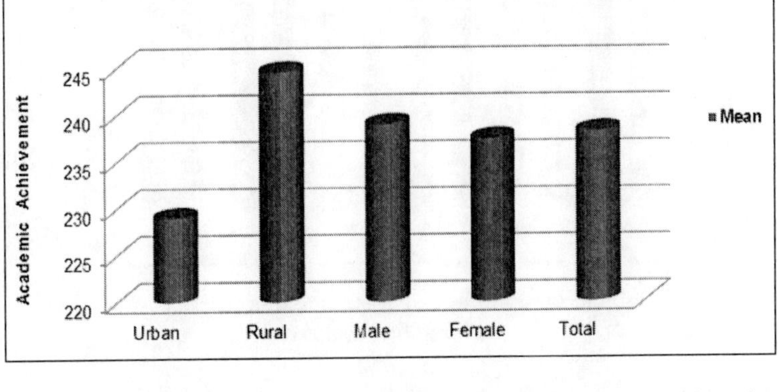

Figure 1. Average academic achievement scores for urban, rural, male, female and for total

It is observed from table 3 and figure 1 that overall average academic achievement scores of students in rural area is higher than urban area while gender difference is negligible.

Subject wise average academic achievement scores of total, urban and rural area are mentioned in Table 4 and Fig. 2.

Table 4. Subject wise average academic achievement scores of total, urban and rural area

Academic achievement Subject wise	Total		Urban		Rural	
	Mean	S.D.	Mean	S.D.	Mean	S.D.
Hindi	42.46	16.27	43.20	16.63	41.96	16.02
English	39.13	12.12	37.09	10.63	40.55	12.88
Sanskrit	43.24	15.92	42.08	15.40	44.05	16.25
Math	30.31	9.81	27.66	9.63	32.15	9.53
Science	45.00	9.71	42.92	10.28	46.53	9.01
Social Science	38.19	12.80	36.32	13.26	39.51	12.32

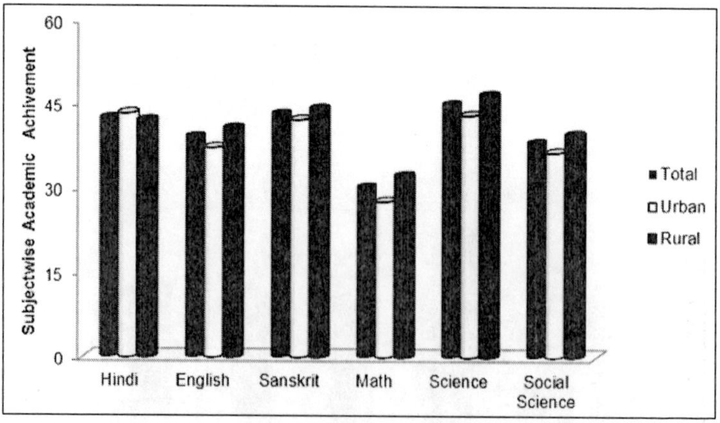

Figure 2. Subject wise average academic achievement scores of total, urban and rural area

It is observed from table 4 and figure 2 that mean value of science achievement is highest in rural area of Chhattisgarh region following the language subjects i.e., Hindi, Sanskrit and English respectively, while mean value of mathematic achievement scores is lowest. In urban areas students were showing high scores in Hindi language only while students residing in rural areas were showing higher achievement than urban students in all subjects excepting Hindi subject.

Subject wise average achievement scores of male and female students (Total) are mentioned in Table 5 and Fig. 3.

Table 5. Subject wise average achievement scores of male and female students (Total)

Academic achievement	Male		Female	
	Mean	S.D.	Mean	S.D.
Hindi	41.79	16.48	43.07	16.07
English	39.59	13.04	38.71	11.22
Sanskrit	42.51	16.54	43.91	15.32
Math	30.79	11.38	29.87	8.1
Science	45.72	10.62	44.43	8.77
Social Science	38.73	13.41	37.70	12.21

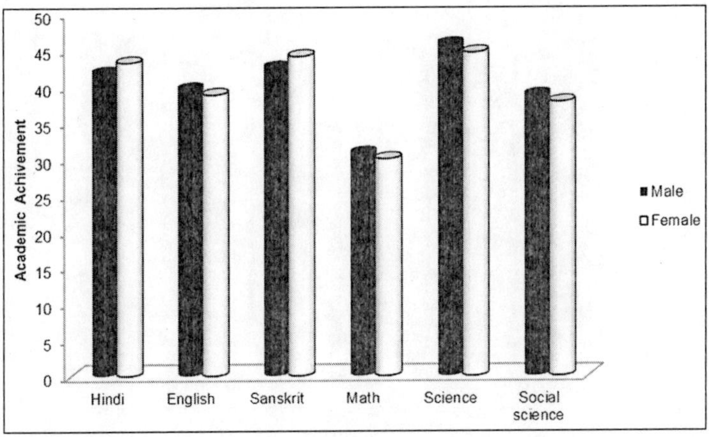

Figure 3. Subject wise average achievement scores of male and female students (Total)

Table 5 and figure 3 indicate that females showed high scores in Hindi and Sanskrit language while males were showing high scores in English language Mathematics, Science and Social Science subjects in Chhattisgarh region.

Subject wise average academic achievement scores for locale and sex are mentioned in Table 6 and Fig. 4 and Fig. 5.

Table 6.
Subject wise average achievement scores for locale and sex

Subjects	Urban		Rural	
	Male	**Female**	**Male**	**Female**
	Mean	*Mean*	*Mean*	*Mean*
Hindi	40.46	45.68	42.72	41.28
English	36.48	37.652	41.74	39.47
Sanskrit	40.03	43.94	44.22	43.89
Math	26.973	28.299	33.45	30.97
Science	43.24	42.622	47.43	45.70
Social science	35.62	36.96	40.90	38.24

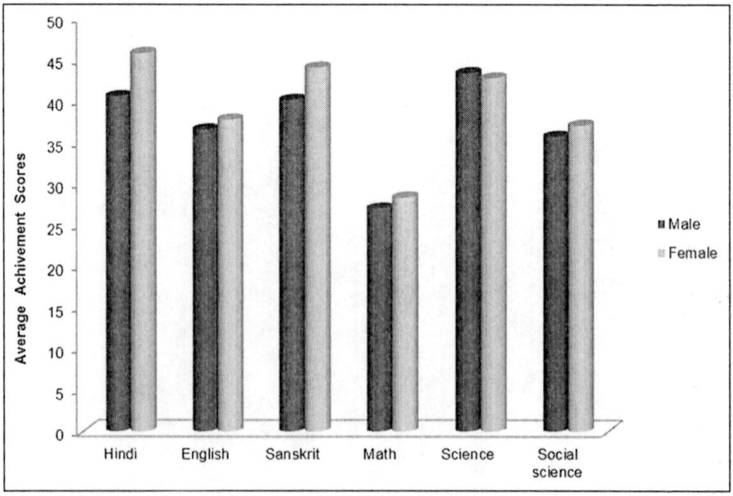

Figure 4. Subject wise average achievement scores (Urban)

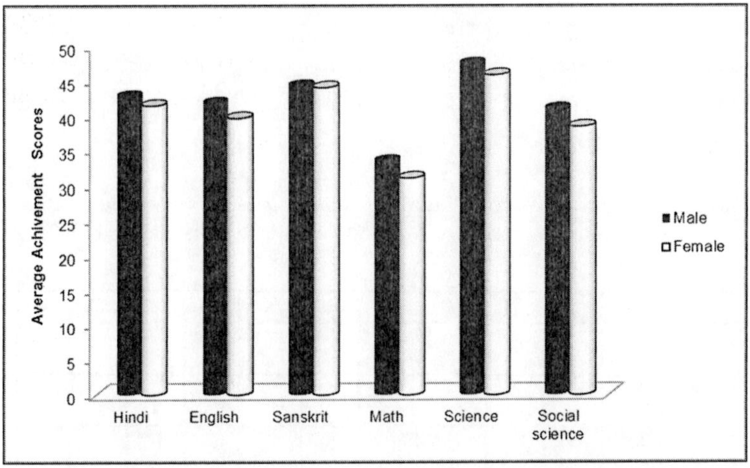

Figure 5. Subject wise average achievement scores (Rural)

It is observed from table 6 and figure 4 that in urban area mean value of female achievement is higher in all subjects than male student except in science subjects.

These results also supported by some other previous researches, which found that females are outperforming males at all levels of the school system, (Alton Lee & Praat, 2001; House of Representatives Standing Committee on Education and Training, 2002; Mullis et. al., 2003; Office for Standards in Education, 2003) Student's gender strongly affects their academic performance, with girls performing better in the subjects of Mathematics, and English as well as cumulatively.

Girls usually show more efforts leading towards better grades at school (Ceballo, Mc Loyd & Toyokawa, 2004). In rural area this trend was seen opposite (fig. 5). Rural male student achievement is higher than female students with respect to all subjects. This may be due to their domestic involvement and their social discouragement and gender discrimination in rural areas.

Coefficient of correlation for academic achievement in relation to classroom environment for total, rural, urban, male, female are mentioned in Table 7 and shown in Fig. 6, 7, 8,9 and 10 respectively.

Table 7. Coefficient of correlation for academic achievement in relation to classroom environment for total, rural, urban, male, female.

Variable	I	Aff	TS	TO	C	O&O	RC	C	Inn	Locale	Sex
Aca. ach. (Total)	.252**	.282**	.162**	.260**	.212**	.198**	.215**	.214**	.024	.077*	-.012
Aca. ach. (Rural)	.279**	.344**	.159*	**.323****	.278**	.291**	.253**	.234**	.018		
Aca.ach. (Urban)	.235**	.185**	.191**	.160**	.107*	.106*	.140*	.201**	.170**		
Aca.ach. (Male)	.181**	.236**	.268**	.188**	.183**	.119*	.149**	.140**	.225**		
Aca.ach. (Female)	.327**	**.332****	.131**	.332**	.243**	.304**	.289**	.287**	.020		

**P <.01 *P < .05

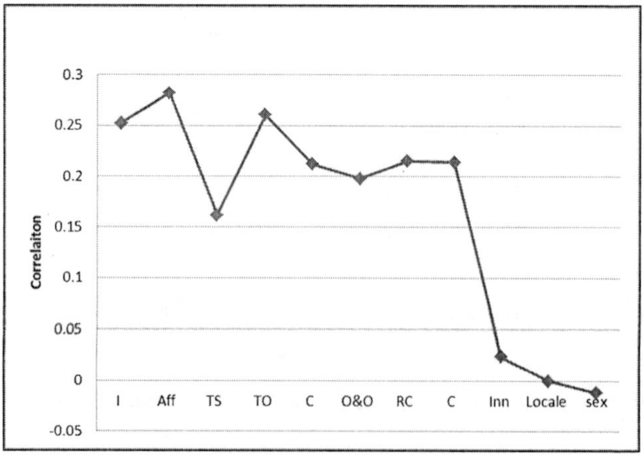

Figure 6. Coefficient of correlation for academic achievement and classroom environment (Total)

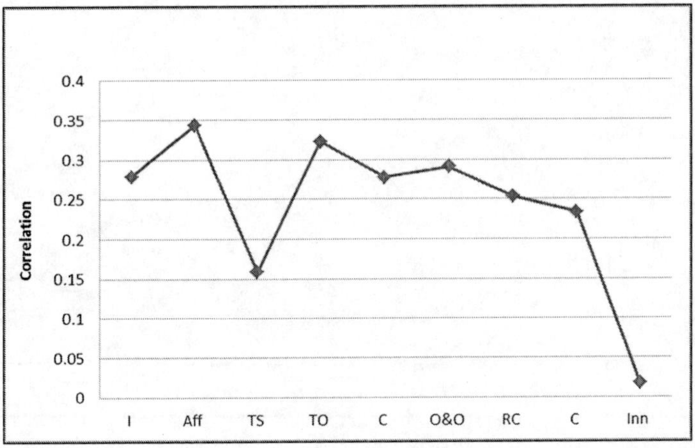

Figure 7. Coefficient of correlation for academic achievement and classroom environment (Rural)

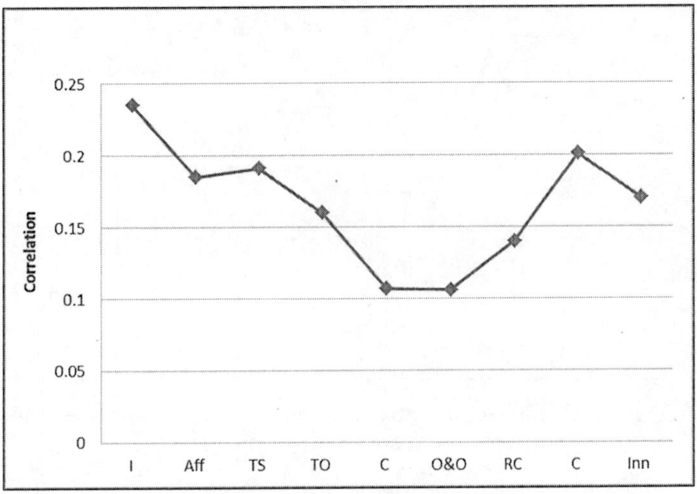

Figure 8. Coefficient of correlation for academic achievement and classroom environment (Urban)

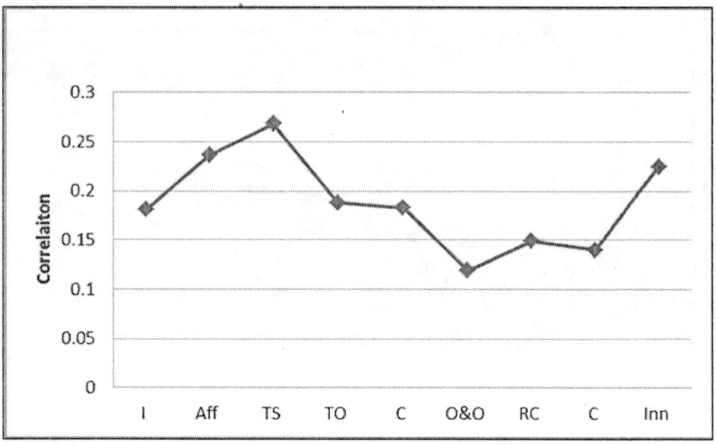

Figure 9. Coefficient of correlation for academic achievement and classroom environment (Male)

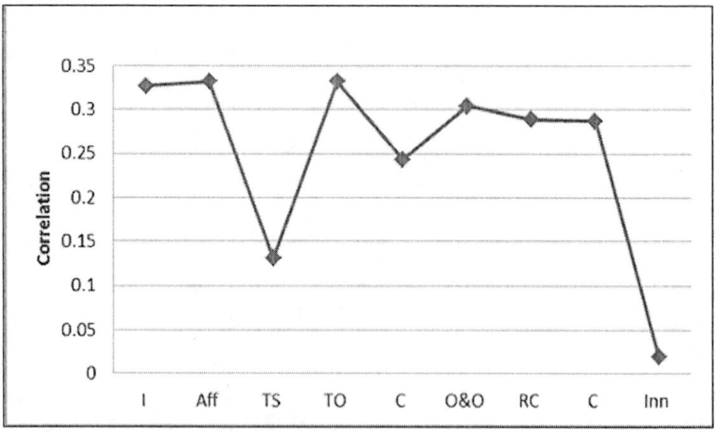

Figure 10. Coefficient of correlation for academic achievement and classroom environment (Female)

It is observed from table 7 and figure 6 that coefficient of correlation for academic achievement of students results were significantly related in a positive direction with all the dimensions of classroom environment namely involvement (I), affiliation (Aff.) teacher support (TS), task orientation (TO), competition(C), order and organization (O & O), rule clarity (RC), teacher control (TC) and innovation (Inn). Results showed that among correlated variables to academic achievement affiliation has the highest correlation ($r = .282$) with academic achievement, followed by task orientation, involvement, rule clarity, teacher control, competition, order and organization, teacher support, innovation and locale (ruralness) respectively. While sex (femininity) has the negative relationship with the academic achievement but the relationship was not found significant.

For rural area results indicated that among correlated variables to academic achievement affiliation has the highest correlation ($r = .344$) and after that task orientation $r = .323$, whereas innovation ($r = .081$) has the lowest correlation.

Result also showed that in rural area coefficient of correlations were seen higher than urban area for all sub dimensions, i.e., involvement, affiliation, task orientation, competition, order and organization, rule clarity, teacher control dimensions, except teacher support and innovation. Table also indicated that females showing high correlation for all sub dimensions of classroom environment except teacher support and innovation sub dimension than males, coefficient of correlation for these two dimensions were high in males. This finding is supported by the study of Huang (2003) indicated that girls perceived their classroom learning environments more positively than boys. Girls were more involved, more affiliated and more cooperative with their classmates than boys.

Role of Classroom Environment and Overall Academic Achievement

The first problem of the present study was to investigate the role of classroom environment in academic achievement of the students. It was hypothesized that classroom environment (along with its dimensions i. e. involvement, affiliation teacher support, task orientation, competition, order organization, rule clarity, teacher control and innovation) would contribute significantly to academic achievement of the student.

Stepwise multiple regression analysis for overall academic achievement scores (Total) are mentioned in Table 8 and shown in Fig. 11.

Table 8. Stepwise multiple regression analysis for overall academic achievement scores (Total)

Predictor variables	R	R^2	R square change	F change	Unstd. b Coeff.	Std. β Coeff.	t	Explained variance
Constant					129.649			
Affiliation	.282a	.079	.079	81.516	1.799	.175	4.598	7.9%
Task Orientation	.307	.094	.015	15.506	1.265	.118	3.061	1.5%
Teacher Control	.318	.101	.007	7.146	1.213	0.98	2.826	.7%
Locale	.328	.108	.007	6.887	7.766	.081	2.624	.7%

$R = .328$, $R^2 = .108$, $F = 28.401$, $P < .01$

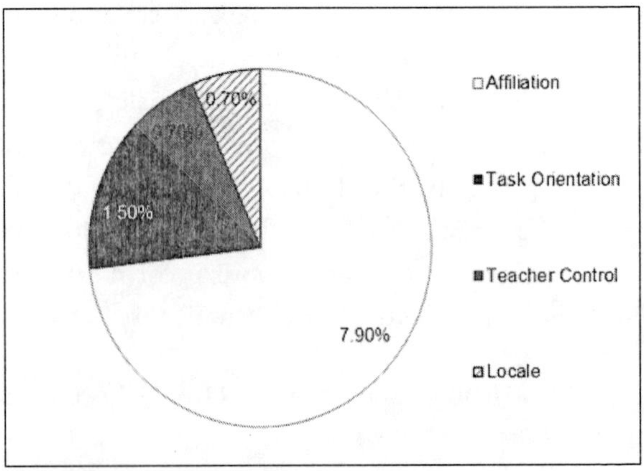

Figure 11. Explained variance in academic achievement of students' by significant variable (Total)

Results of stepwise multiple regression analysis for academic achievement reveals that the model of regression analysis is significant, as the R square =.108, F= 28.401, p<.01 indicates the strength of model. It is observed that 10.8% variance of I. V. taken in total is contributed significantly in the variation of the criterion variable academic achievement. The affiliation, task orientation, teacher control sub-dimensions of classroom environment and locale emerge out to be significant predictors contributing significantly in the variation of criterion variable academic achievement whereas the other remaining variables i. e., involvement, teacher support, competition, order and organization, rule clarity and innovation were not found to be significant in explaining variance of academic achievement. The beta coefficient of significant variables indicated that the affiliation sub dimension of classroom environment was the most important predictor emerged out and explained alone 7.9% of variance in students academic achievement. Affiliation assesses the level of friendship student feel for each other i.e., the extent to which they help each other with homework, get to know each other easily and working together.

The second significant variable was the task orientation with beta coefficient of. 118 and it had explained 1.5% of variance of achievement. Task orientation measures the extent to which it is important to complete the activities that have been planned.

The third significant variable was teacher control with beta coefficient of. 098 and had explained. 7% of variance of achievement. It measures how strict the teacher is in enforcing the rules and the severity of the punishment for rule infractions.

The fourth significant variable was locale with beta coefficient of. 081 and it had explained. 7% of variance of achievement.

The findings of this study supported by the findings of earlier researches viz. Anderson *et. al.*, (2004); Chua, (2004); Davis, (2004); which found that there was a significant relationship between students perceptions of classroom environment i.e., involvement, affiliation, teacher support, task orientation, order and organization, and rule clarity and their outcomes.

Lau Shiao Wei (2011) found affiliation as the most important dimension of classroom environment, Welberg and Haertel's (1981) found that student outcomes were enhanced in classes with greater affiliation and task orientation. Goh and Khine (2002) have mentioned that a good teacher student relationship is superior to the creation and maintenance of a positive classroom. Eshel and Kohavi (2003) found that academic achievement would be highest when student and teacher control is high, and would be lowest when both of them are low. Kiany (2011) studied high school students perceptions of teacher control orientations and their English achievement and found that teacher control had a statistically significant effect on student outcomes.

In the present study role of locale was found to be significant and it shows that ruralness may enhance academic achievement. This finding does not support the findings of earlier researches by Nagaraju *et. al.,* (2003); Usha, (2007); Joshi, and Shrivastava, (2009) which found that the achievement of the pupils from urban areas was better than the achievement of pupils from rural areas. Some of the studies give contradictory findings that there is no significant difference in the academic performance of students from rural and urban environment by Alokan, Funmilola, Bosede, Arijesuyo and Amos Emiloju (2013); Wobmann (2010). This may be due to the educational awareness of people from rural area performing better than urban area. One of the reasons may be the sample of the present study which was taken only from government schools.

We know that in urban area every parent wants their ward should be educated from reputed school. They have many options for their schooling, private schooling of children became as status symbol for parents. In such conditions in urban area only those parents belongs to low socio economic status send their ward in government school, in contrast in rural area parents have no such options.

Results Regarding Subject Wise Academic Achievement Scores (Total)

To find out the best predictors for subject wise achievement, subject wise multiple regression analysis was carried out. Table 8 shows analysis of the data for Hindi subject the multiple co relational co-efficient was found to be. 320 which was highly significant, P <. 01) its R square was. 102, which indicated that the significant variables included in the present analysis contributed 10.2% variance in the Hindi subject achievement scores of the students.

The beta coefficient of significant variables indicated that the teacher support and involvement sub dimensions of classroom environment were the most important dimensions emerged out and explained 7.0% and 1.9% of variation of Hindi achievement respectively. For English subject the multiple co relational co-efficient was found to be. 323 which was highly significant (F = 27.46, P <. 01) its R square was. 105 which indicated that the significant variables included in the present analysis contributed 10.5% variance in the English achievement scores of the students. The beta coefficient of significant variables indicated that the affiliation, teacher support, competition sub dimensions of classroom environment and locale (ruralness) were the most important variable emerged out and explained 6.8%, 2.2%, 0.6% and 0.8% variation of English achievement respectively. For achievement of Sanskrit subject the multiple co relational co-efficient was found to be. 331 which was highly significant (F = 28.91 P <. 01) its R square was. 109 which indicated that the significant variables included in the present analysis contributed 10.9% variance of Sanskrit achievement scores of the students.

The beta coefficient of significant variables indicated that the teacher support, task orientation, affiliation sub dimensions of classroom environment and femininity (sex) were the most important variable emerged out and explained 7.9% and 1.9%, 0.6% and 0.5% of variation of Sanskrit achievement respectively. For achievement of Mathematics subject model of regression analysis is significant as the R square =.088, F= 22.675, p<. 01, which indicates strength of the model, its R square value=. 088 which indicated that significant variables included in the present analysis contributed 8.8%of variance in academic achievement.

Analysis shows that b coefficient for three factors namely affiliation, teacher support, and teacher control was found to be significant and had explained 4.3%, 1.2% and 0.6% of variance of mathematics achievement respectively, whereas the other remaining variables were found to be insignificant in explaining variance of mathematics achievement. For achievement of science subject regression model is significant with R= .229, R^2= .084, F= 21.54. Beta coefficient for affiliation, teacher support and teacher control was found to be significant and had explained 5.2%, 0.9% and 0.5% of variance. For social science subject the model is significant with R= .321, R^2 = 10.3, F= 27.04, P<=.01 which indicates the strength of model. Its R square value .103 indicated that significant variables included in the present analysis contributed 10.3% of variance in academic achievement.

Teacher support emerged out as most significant predictor for their achievement and explained 6.9% of variance for social science achievement. Table 9 shows that teacher support sub dimension of classroom environment was the most important predictor emerged out significantly for achievement of all subjects and explained. 7.0%, (Hindi), 2.2% (English), 7.9% (Sanskrit), 1.2% (Mathematics). 9% (Science) and 6.9% of variance of Social Science achievement. Teacher support measures the amount of help, concern and friendship the teacher directs toward the students. Student perception of teacher support have been associated with greater feelings of school belonging (Ma, 2003, Osterman, 2000) and greater school engagement and motivation as well as better academic performance (Birch & Ladd, 1998) positive teacher-student relationship were associated with better school performance (Chiaki Konishi, 2010). Affiliation was the second important dimension emerged out as significant factor and explained 6.8% (English), 6% (Sanskrit), 4.3% (Mathematics), 5.2% (Science) and 1.9% of Social Science achievement.

Results regarding stepwise multiple regression for subject wise achievement are presented in Table 9 and explained variance in subject wise achievement of students by significant variable are shown in Fig. 12a, 12b, 12c, 12d, 12e, 12f respectively.

Table 9. Stepwise multiple regression analysis for subject wise achievement (Total)

Significant Variable	Hindi			English			Sanskrit			Math			Science			Social Science		
	b	β	*Exp. Vari.*	*b*	β	*Exp. Vari.*	*b*	β	*Exp. Vari.*	*b*	β	*Exp. Vari.*	*b*	β	*Exp. Vari.*	*b*	β	Exp. Vari.
(CONSTANT)	13.759			19.11						14.991			30.258			16.830		
I	0.320	0.131	1.9%															
A				.274	.144	6.8%	.263	.105	.6%	.188	.122	4.3%	.229	.150	5.2%	.259	.129	1.9 %
TS	0.583	0.174	7.0%	.384	.154	2.2%	.571	.174	7.9%	.223	.110	1.2%	.194	.097	0.9%	.434	.165	6.9 %
TO							.308	.118	1.9%									
C				.234	.091	.6%												
O&O																		
RC																		
TC	.314	.102	.7%							.155	.083	.6%	.146	.079	.5%	.249	.102	0.8 %
Inn.																		
Gender	2..523	.077	.6%				2.32 9	.073	.5%									
Locale				1.63 5	.092	.8%				2.408	.167	2.7%	1.893	.132	1.7%	1.586	.084	0.7 %
	R=.320, R2=10.2 F=26.885, P<.01			R=.323, R2=10.5 F=27.46, P<.01			R=.331, R2=10.9 F=28.91, P<.01			R=.296, R2=8.8 F=22.675, P<.01			R=.229, R2=8.4 F=21.54, P<.01			R=.321, R2=10.3 F=27.04, P<.01		

b = b Coefficient β = β Coefficient Exp. Vari. = Explained Variance

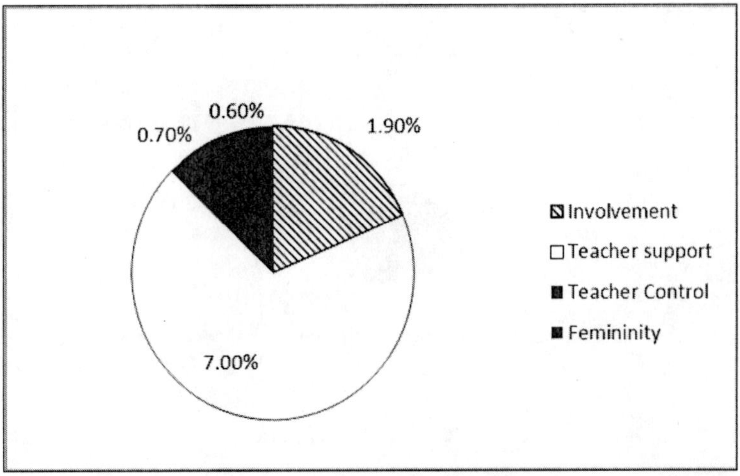

Figure 12(a). Explained variance by significant variable for Hindi subject achievement (Total)

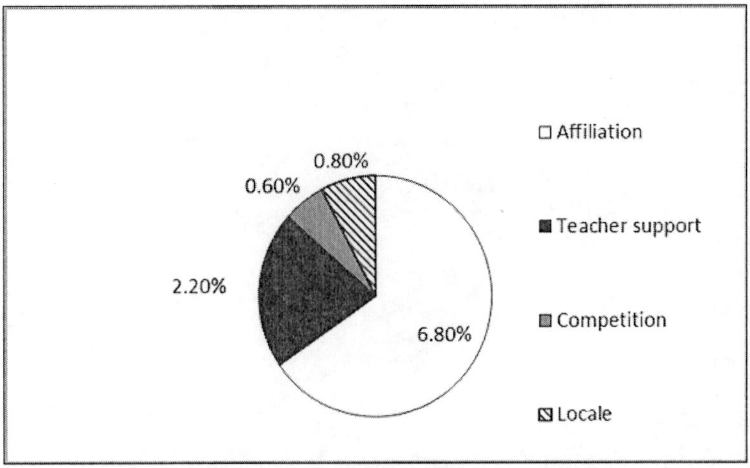

Figure 12(b). Explained variance by significant variable for English subject achievement (Total)

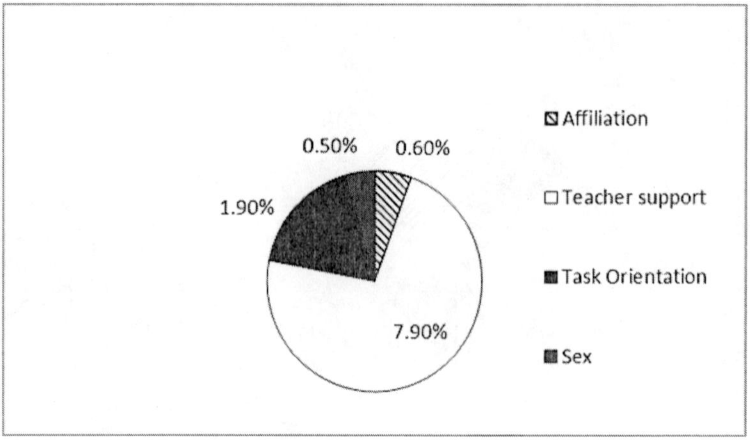

Figure 12(c). Explained variance by significant variable for Sanskrit subject achievement (Total)

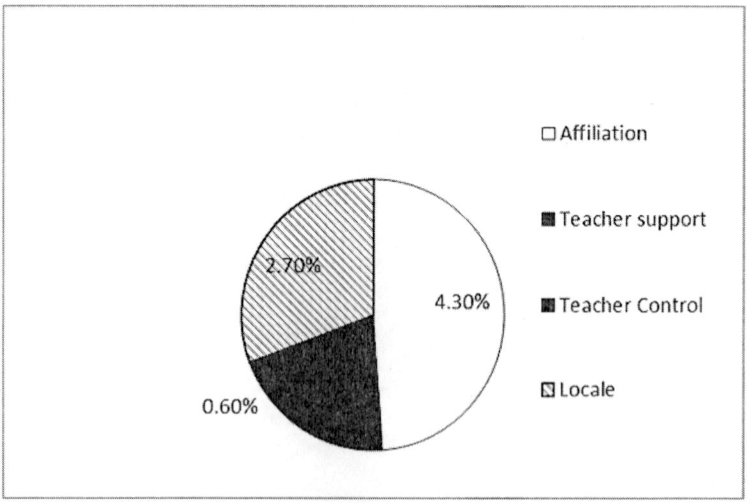

Figure 12(d). Explained variance by significant variable for Mathematics subject achievement (Total)

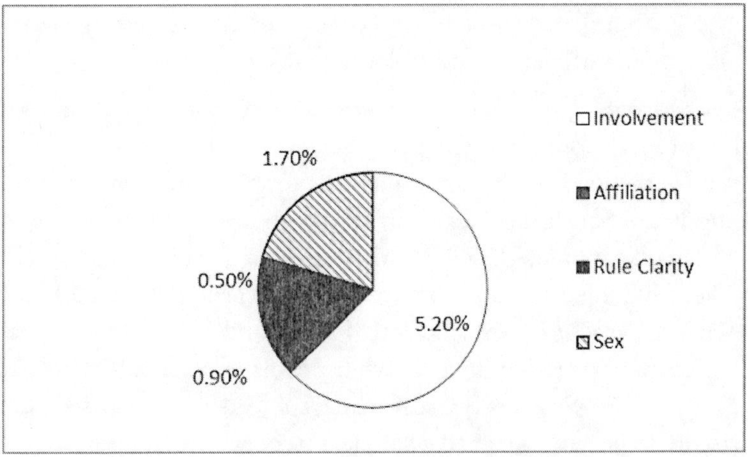

Figure 12(e). Explained variance by significant variable for Science subject achievement (Total)

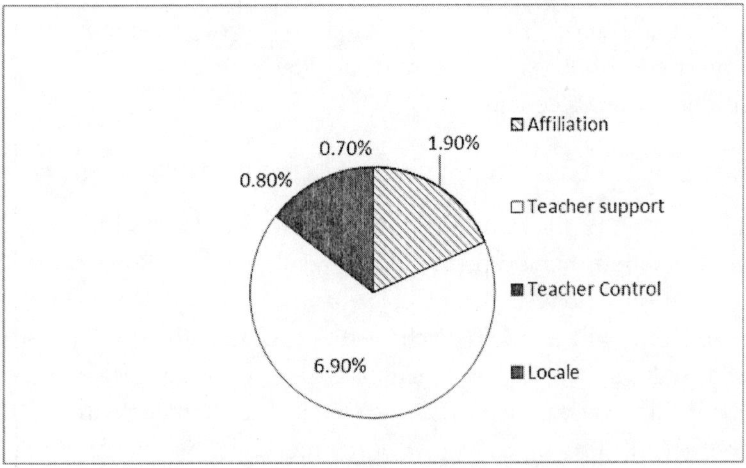

Figure 12(f). Explained variance by significant variable for Social Science subject achievement (Total)

Findings of Wei and Elias & (2011) supported these results that affiliation is the most important dimension of classroom environment for their achievement, Welberg and Haertel's

(1981) found that student outcomes were enhanced in classes with greater affiliation and task orientation.

Results also shows that teacher control dimension was important for mathematics, science and social science achievements. Role of femininity was found to be significant for Hindi and Sanskrit subjects while role of ruralness was found to be significant for English, Mathematics, Science and Social Science subjects. It shows that in government schools of Chhattisgarh achievement of Hindi and Sanskrit subjects increased with femininity, while achievement of English, Mathematics, Science, Social Science subjects was increased with ruralness because of rural awareness in education.

Thus, we find that the hypotheses stating that classroom environment along with its various dimensions i.e. involvement, affiliation teacher support, task orientation, competition, order and organization, rule clarity, teacher control and innovation, would contribute significantly to academic achievement of the students were accepted.

ROLE OF LOCALE AND OVERALL ACADEMIC ACHIEVEMENT

The second problem of the study was to see the role of locale in academic achievement. The results of coefficient of correlation showed that locale has the significant positive correlation with academic achievement of the students. Results of multiple regression analysis showed that locale play significant role to determine academic achievement with beta coefficient. 081 and it had explained .7% of variance of achievement. Results also indicated that in male students locale plays the significant role to predict academic achievement with beta coefficient of .187 and it had explained 2.7% of variance of academic achievement. For female student locale was not found as significant predictor.

ROLE OF LOCALE AND SUBJECT WISE ACHIEVEMENT

In order to investigate the role of locale and subject wise achievement, it was found significant for English, Mathematics, Science and Social Science subjects. It showed that achievement of English, Mathematics, Science and Social Science subjects was increased with ruralness because of rural awareness in education. It may be concluded that ruralness may enhance academic achievement. In the present study role of locale was found to be significant and it shows that ruralness may enhance academic achievement, this finding does not supported the findings of earlier researches by Joshi, and Shrivastava, (2009); Nagaraju *et. al.,* (2003); Usha, (2007) which found that the achievement of the pupils from urban areas was better than the achievement of pupils from rural areas. Some of the studies give contradictory findings that there is no significant difference in the academic performance of students from rural and urban environment by Alokan, Funmilola Bosede and Arijesuyo, Amos Emiloju (2013) and Wobmann (2010). This may be due to the educational awareness of people from rural area performing better than urban area. One of the reasons may be the sample of the present study as it was mentioned earlier in chapter four that the sample of the study which was taken only from state government schools. We know that in urban area every parent wants their ward should be educated from a reputed school. They have many options for their schooling, private schooling of children became as status symbol for parents. In such conditions in urban area only those parents belong to low socio economic status send their ward in government school. In contrast parents belong to rural area have no such options.

In male students role of locale was found significant for English, Mathematics, Science and Social Science subjects and it had explained 2.9% variance of English achievement, 7.9% variance of mathematic achievement, 3.0% variance of science achievement and 2.9% variance of social science achievement.

In female students role of locale was found to be significant for Hindi, Mathematics and Science achievement with Beta Coefficient -.099, .096 and .105 respectively, it explained 0.8% variance of Hindi achievement, 0.9% variance of Mathematics achievement and 1.0% variance of Science achievement. Here the negative nature of beta coefficient for Hindi subject indicated that the achievement of Hindi became less favorable with the increase in ruralness. This shows that ruralness is less favorable for Hindi achievement in female students this may be due to the effect of local language.

Overall Academic Achievement of Rural Student

To find out the best predictors of academic achievement in rural areas separate regression analysis for rural students was carried out. Results regarding stepwise multiple regression analysis of academic achievement of rural students were presented in table 10 and figure 13.

It is observed from Table 10 that model of regression analysis for academic achievement of rural students was found to be significant as the R = .386, R Square = .149, F= 32.279, P<.01 which indicated significant strength of the model. Model shows that the significant variables included in the present analysis contributed to 14.9% of variance in determining the academic achievement of the rural students. The affiliation, task orientation and competition, sub dimension of classroom environment emerge out to be significant predictors contributing significantly in the variation of criterion variable. Table 10 also shows that in rural area affiliation task orientation and competitions factors play significant role in determining achievement whereas it was insignificant in urban area. This indicated that the increase in the affiliation, task orientation and competition increases the academic achievement of the rural students.

Table 10. Stepwise multiple regression analysis for overall academic achievement of rural students

Predictor variable	R	R2	R square change	F change	Unstd. b coeff.	Std. β Coeff.	t	Explained Variance
Constant					141.440		18.839	
Affiliation	.344a	.119	.119	74.777	1.789	.195	3.784	11.9%
Task Orientation	.375b	.141	.022	14.291	1.601	.160	3.220	2.2%
Competition.	.386c	.149	.008	5.281	1.339	.107	2.298	.8%

R = .386, R^2 = .149, F = 32.279, P <.01 D. V.: Academic achievement

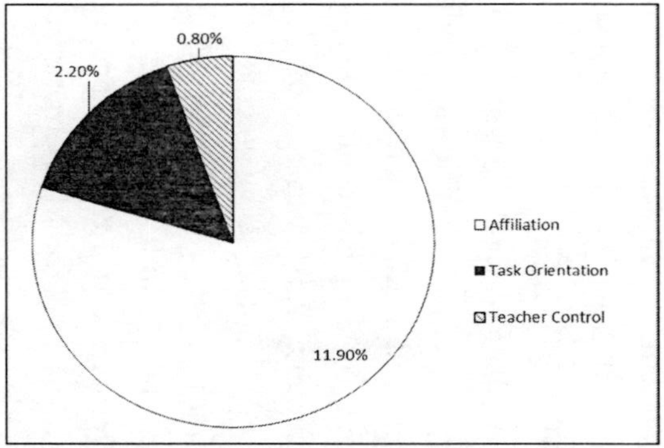

Figure 13. Explained variance in academic achievement of students' by significant variable (Rural)

SUBJECT WISE ACADEMIC ACHIEVEMENT OF RURAL STUDENTS

Results showed that in rural students teacher support was the most important factor emerged out as significant predictor for subject wise achievements. beta co-efficient showed that it had explained alone 9.5% variance of Hindi achievement, 10.0% variance of English achievement, 9.3% variance of Sanskrit achievement, 5.9% variance of math achievement 2.1% of variance of science achievement and 10.3% variance of social science achievement.

Affiliation was the second important factor which was emerged out as significant predictor for English, Sanskrit, Science and Social Science achievement and explained 2.4% variance of English achievement, 2.7% variance of Sanskrit achievement, 9.4% variance of Science achievement and 2.3% variance of Social science achievement. Competition dimension was found to be significant predictor for English and Math Achievement and Explained 1.0% variance of English achievement and 1.8% variance of Math achievement. Result also shows that for Mathematic subject sex play the significant role with beta coefficient of -.101and had explained 1.0% of variance of Math achievement. Here the negative nature indicated that the achievement of mathematic became less favorable with the increase in femininity. This shows that if subject will be feminine the achievement of mathematics will be lower.

Results regarding stepwise multiple regression for subject wise achievement of rural students are presented in Table-11 and Explained variance in subject wise achievement of students by significant variable are shown in Fig. 14a, 14b, 14c, 14d, 14e, 14f respectively.

Table 11.
Stepwise multiple regression for subject wise achievement (Rural)

Significant Variable	Hindi			English			Sanskrit			Math			Science			Social Science		
	b	β	Exp. Vari.	b	β	Exp. Vari.	b	β	Exp. Vari.	b	β	Exp. Vari.	b	β	Exp. Vari.	b	β	Exp. Vari.
(CONSTANT)	18.28 6			20.34 5						24.774			34.340					
I																		
A				.249	.135	2.4%	.319	.137	2.7%				.276	.214	9.4%	.319	.181	2.3%
TS	.670	.212	9.5%	.508	.201	10.%	.522	.163	9.3%	.339	.181	5.9%	.304	.172	2.1%	.542	.224	10.3%
TO	.464	.185	2.5%				.330	.130	1.0%									
C				.298	.118	1.0%				.274	.147	1.8%						
O&O																		
RC																		
TC																		
Inn.																		
Gender										-1.930	-.101	1.0%						
Locale																		
	R = .347 R2 = .120 F = 37.939 P < .01			R = .371 R2 = .138 F = 29.398 P < .01			R = .359 R2 = .129.9 F = 27.406 P < .01			R = .276 R2 = .86 F = 22.94 P < .01			R = .338 R2 = .115 F = 35.883 P < .01			R = .355 R2 = .126 F = 39.909 P < .01		

b = b Coefficient β= β Coefficient Exp. Vari. = Explained Variance

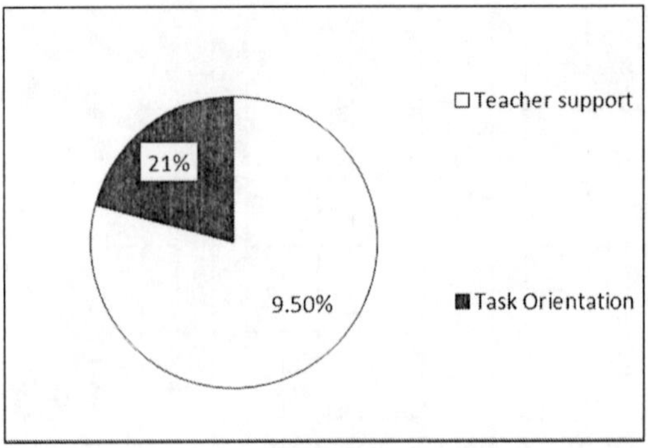

Figure 14(a). Explained variance by significant variable for Hindi subject achievement (Rural)

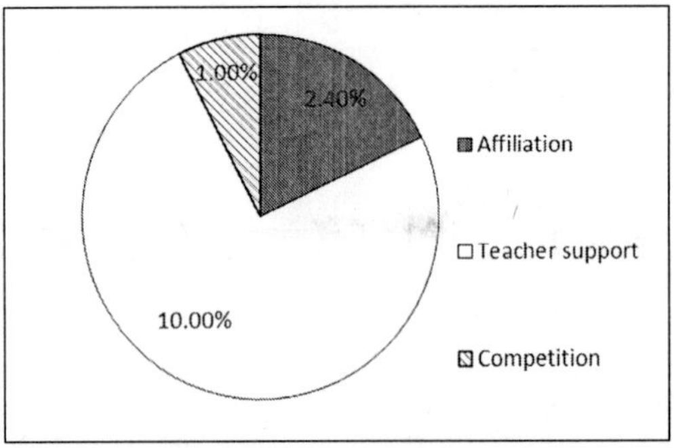

Figure 14 (b). Explained variance by significant variable for English subject achievement (Rural)

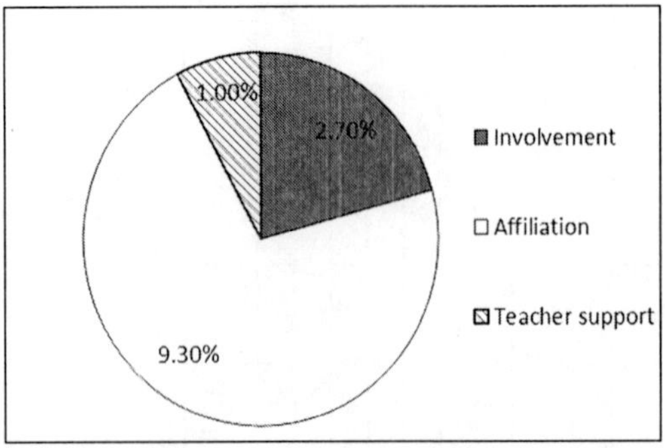

Figure 14 (c). Explained variance by significant variable for Sanskrit subject achievement (Rural)

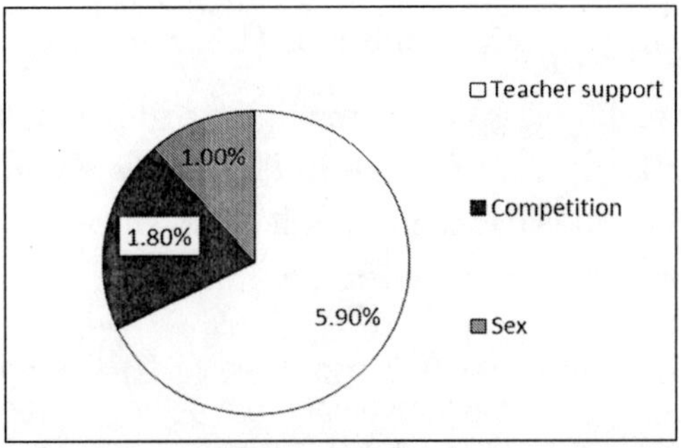

Figure 14 (d). Explained variance by significant variable for Mathematics subject achievement (Rural)

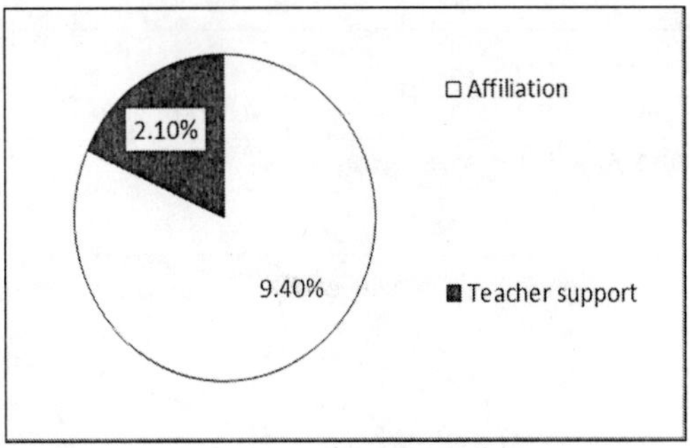

Figure 14 (e). Explained variance by significant variable for Science subject achievement (Rural)

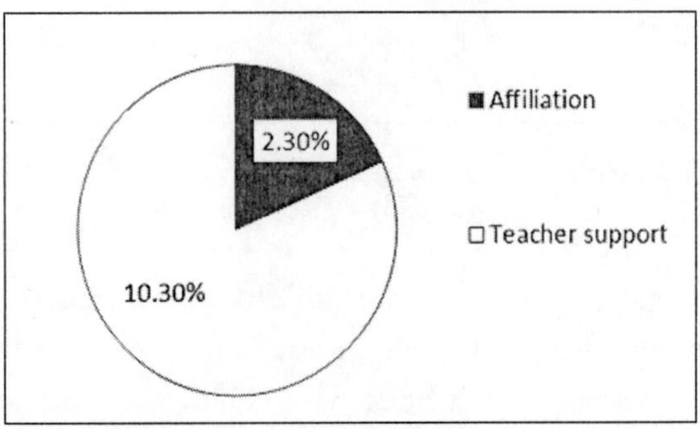

Figure 14 (f). Explained variance by significant variable for Social Science subject achievement (Rural)

Overall Academic Achievement of Urban Students

Results regarding stepwise multiple regression for overall academic achievement of urban students are presented in Table-12 and Explained variance in overall achievement of students by significant variable are shown in Fig. 15.

Table 12. Stepwise multiple regression analysis of academic achievement (urban)

Predictor variable	R	R^2	R square change	F change	Unstd. b. Coeff.	Std. β Coeff.	t	Explained variance
Constant					107.03		5.257	
Involvement	.235a	0.055	0.055	22.679	2.176	0.205	4.004	5.50%
Teacher Control	.273b	0.074	0.019	7.886	2.048	0.152	2.986	1.90%
Sex	.301c	0.091	0.016	6.916	17.019	0.129	2.63	1.60%

R = .301, R^2 = 091 F= 12.786, P<.01 D.V.: Academic achievement

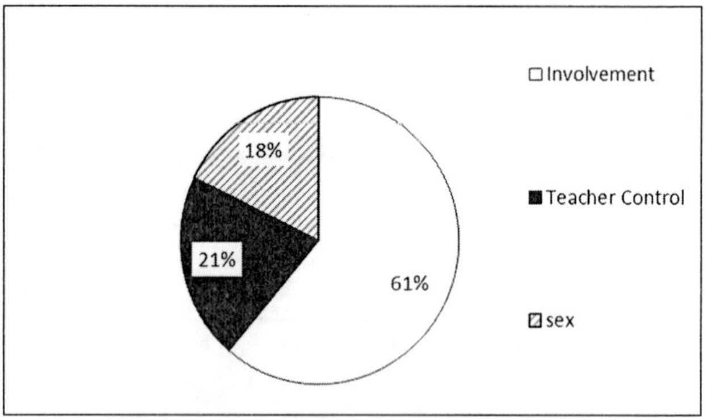

Figure 15. Explained variance in academic achievement of students' by significant variable (Urban)

Results regarding stepwise multiple regression for subject wise achievement of urban students are presented in Table 13 and Explained variance in subject wise achievement of students by significant variable are shown in Fig. 16a, 16b, 16c, 16d, 16e, 16f respectively.

Table 13. Stepwise multiple regression for subject wise achievement (urban)

Significant variable	Hindi			English			Sanskrit			Math			Science			Social Science		
	b	β	Exp. Vari.	b	β	Exp. Vari.	b	β	Exp. Vari.	b	β	Exp. Vari.	b	β	Exp. Vari.	b	β	Exp. Vari.
(CONSTANT)	9.144			25.35			20.22			17.503			36.808			18.74		
I	.522	.195	4.9%	.263	.154	3.5%	.457	.184	6.4%							.407	.190	5.3%
A										.264	.149	3.4%						
TS							.544	.159	2.1%									
TO																		
C																		
O&O																		
RC																		
TC	.544	.163	2.4%	.254	.117	1.3%				.204	.104	1.0%	.320	.153	2.3%	.363	.134	1.6%
Inn.																		
Gender	6.44	.194	3.3%															
Locale																		
	R = .327 R2 = .107 F = 15.35 P < .01			R = .219 R2 = .048 F = 9.67 P < .01			R = .291 R2 = .084 F = 17.813 P < .01			R = .208 R2 = .043 F = 8.71 P<.01			R = .153 R2 = .023 F = 9.223 P<.01			R = .263 R2 = .069 F = 14.339 P<.01		

b = b Coefficient β = β Coefficient Exp. Vari. = Explained Variance

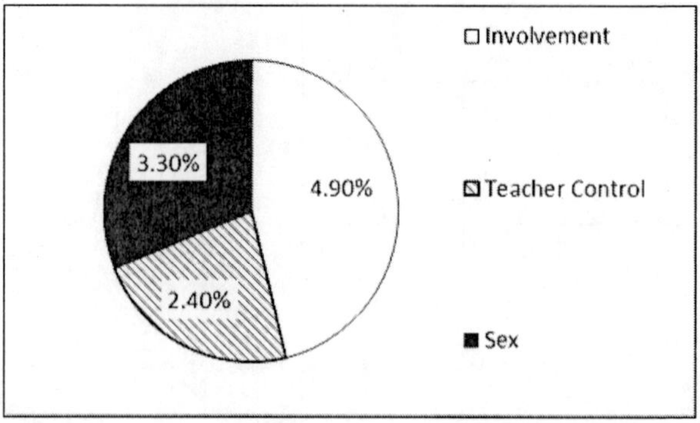

Figure 16(a). Explained variance by significant variable for Hindi subject achievement (Urban)

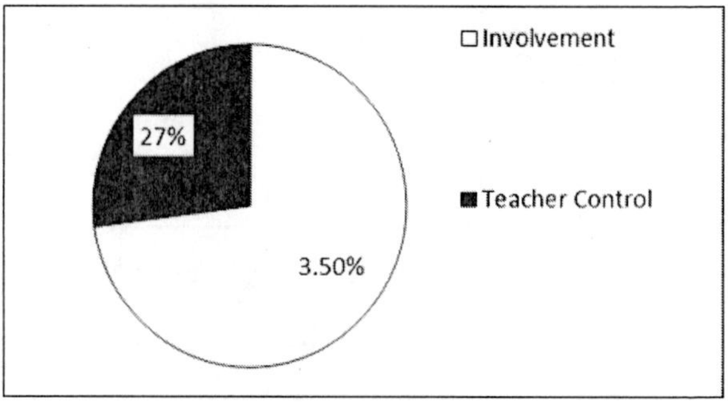

Figure 16(b). Explained variance by significant variable for English subject achievement (Urban)

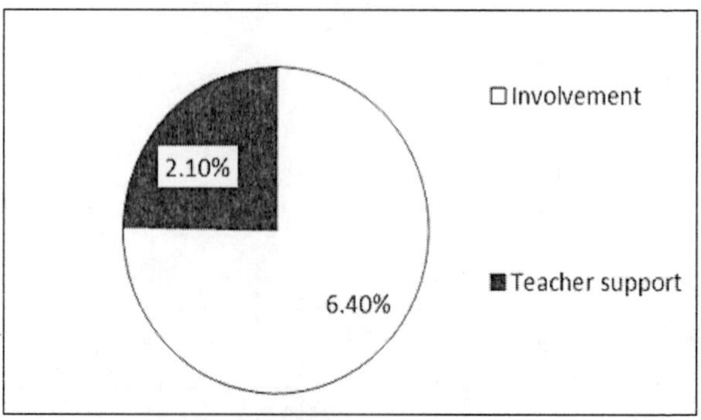

Figure 16(c). Explained variance by significant variable for Sanskrit subject achievement (Urban)

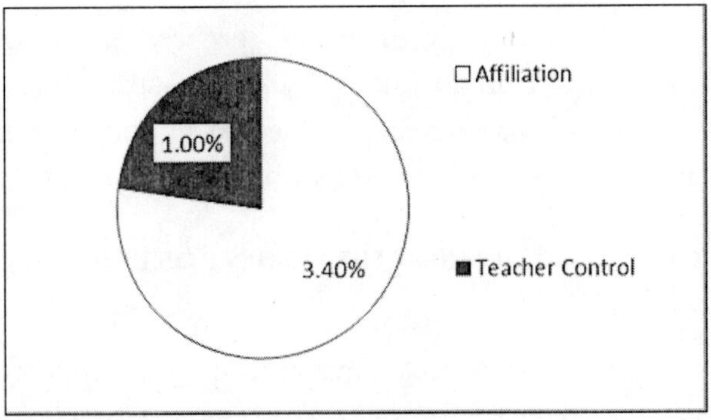

Figure 16(d). Explained variance by significant variable for Mathematics subject achievement (Urban)

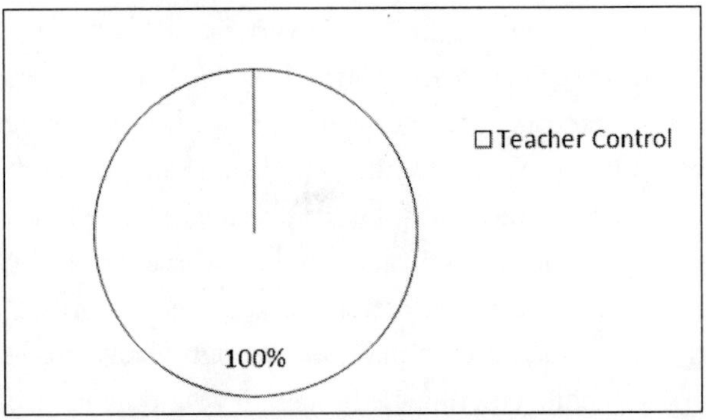

Figure 16(e). Explained variance by significant variable for Science subject achievement (Urban)

In urban students the model of regression analysis showed multiple co relational coefficient for urban students was found to be .301 which was significant with F=12.786, p<.01) R square .091 which indicated that significant variables included in the present analysis contributed to 9.1% of variance in determining the achievement of the students. In urban area involvement, teacher control sub dimension of classroom environment and sex emerged out to be significant predictors contributing significantly in the variation of criterion variable. It shows that the increase in the involvement and teacher control increased the achievement of urban students. In urban area femininity has the significant role to determine achievement; it indicates that in urban area achievement increases with femininity.

SUBJECT WISE ACADEMIC ACHIEVEMENT OF URBAN STUDENTS

Table 14 shows that in urban area teacher control emerged out as significant predictor for subject wise achievements, beta co-efficient shows that it had explained alone 2.4% variance of Hindi achievement, 1.3% variance of English achievement, 1.0% variance of Math achievement 2.3% of variance of science achievement and 1.6% variance of social science achievement. Results also pointed out that in urban area involvement factor emerged out as significant predictor for language subject's i. e. Hindi, English, Sanskrit and it had explained 4.9%, variance of Hindi achievement, 3.5% variance of English achievement and 6.4% variance of Sanskrit achievement while for mathematics, science and social science teacher control factor emerged out as significant predictor for subject wise achievements. Data also reveal that in urban area femininity has the significant role for Hindi achievement and it had explained 3.3% variance of Hindi achievement this shows that the achievement of Hindi subject increases with femininity in urban area.

Thus we find that the hypotheses stating that locale would contribute significantly to academic achievement of the students was accepted.

Role of Sex and Overall Academic Achievement

Another problem of the present study was to see the role of sex in academic achievement. Result of coefficient of correlation shows that sex has the negative correlation with academic achievement of the students but it was not found significant. Results of stepwise multiple regression analysis showed that role of sex was not found significant for total population findings confirm by earlier researchers. (Arigbabu & Mji 2004; Bilesanmi-Awoderu, 2006; David & Stanley, 2000; Din, Ming, & Esther, 2004; Fakeye (2010); Freedman, 2002; Gupta, Sharma and Gupta (2012); Pandey and Ahmad (2008); Sungur and Tekkaya, 2003; Tella *et. al.,* (2010) etc.) which found no significant difference in academic achievement of students with respect to gender.

Results also pointed out that in urban areas femininity has the significant role to determine academic achievement with beta coefficient of .129 and it had explained 1.6%of variance of academic achievement of urban students while trend was opposite for rural areas.

Possible reason may be due to the parental awareness about female child education. Findings supported by earlier researchers (Alton Lee & Praat 2001; House of Representatives Standing Committee on Education and Training, 2002; Mullis *et. al.,* 2003; Office for Standards in Education, 2003).

In rural areas role of femininity was not seen significant. This may be due to the, social evils i.e. gender discrimination, lack of motivation from parents, responsibilities of house hold work in early age, lack of awareness of parents, lack of interest about female child education, and mentality of early marriage, femininity was not associated with achievement in rural are.

Role of Sex and Subject Wise Academic Achievement

In order to investigate the role of sex and subject wise achievement it was found to be significant for Hindi and Sanskrit subjects only and it had explained .6% and .5% of variance in achievement of respective subject. In urban area role of sex was found to be significant for Hindi subject only. In rural area femininity has the negative role for mathematic achievement.

It may be said that if subject will be feminine (girls) the achievement of mathematic will be lower in rural area while in urban area if subject will be feminine (girls) achievement of Hindi will be enhance.

Academic Achievement of Male Students

Results regarding stepwise multiple regression analysis of academic achievement of male students were presented in Table 14 and figure 17.

Table 14.
Stepwise multiple regression analysis of academic achievement (Male)

Predictor Variable	R	R2	R square change	F change	Unstd. b Coeff.	Std. β Coeff.	t	Explained variance
Constant					82.569		4.198	
Teacher Support	.268a	.072	.072	34.766	2.485	.165	3.311	7.2
Locale	.315b	.099	.027	13.661	26.886	.187	4.180	2.7%
Affiliation	.347c	.120	.021	10.627	1.529	.128	2.499	2.1%
Competition	.361	.130	.010	5.258	1.764	.110	2.293	1.0%

R= .361, R^2 = .130 F = 16.734, P<.01 D.V.: academic achievement

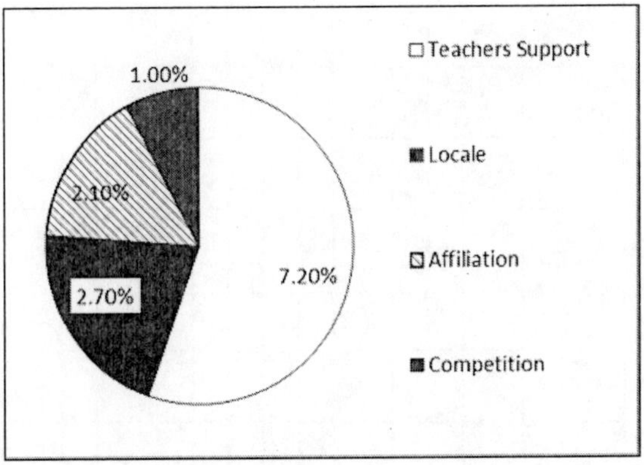

Figure 17: Explained variance in academic achievement of students' by significant variable (Male)

To find out the best predictors in male students for academic achievement, the separate stepwise multiple regression analysis for academic achievement of male students was carried out, Table shows analysis of the data that the multiple corelational co-efficient was found to be .361 which was highly significant (F=16.73, P<.000) its R square was .130,which indicated that the significant variables included in the present analysis contributed 13.9% variance in the achievement scores of the students. The teacher support, affiliation, competition sub dimension of classroom environment and locale emerge out to be significant predictors contributing significantly in the variation of criterion variable academic achievement. Whereas remaining variables were found to be insignificant in explaining variance of achievement scores of the students.

Results regarding stepwise multiple regression for subject wise achievement of male students are presented in Table 15 and Explained variance in subject wise achievement of students by significant variable are shown in Fig. 18a, 18b, 18c, 18d, 18e, 18f respectively.

Table 15. Stepwise multiple regression for subject wise achievement (Male)

Significant variable	Hindi			English			Sanskrit			Math			Science			Social science		
	b	β	Exp. Vari.	b	β	Exp. Vari.	b	β	Exp. Vari.	b	β	Exp. Vari.	b	β	Exp. Vari.	b	β	Exp. Vari.
(CONSTANT)	22.551			13.872			11.199			6.017			24.944			10.077		
I																		
A							.359	.129	1.7%	.199	.104	3.6%	.206	.115	1.0%	.303	.134	2.1
TS	.569	.162	4.9 %	.561	.202	6.7%	.511	.145	6.9%	.248.	.102	0.8%	.233	.103	4.1%	.380	.133	5.5%
TO																		
C				.428	.145	1.9%				.294	.114	1.4%	.277	.115	1.9%			
O&O																		
RC																		
TC																		
Inn.	.510	.124	1.2 %				.429	.104	.8%							.319	.112	1.2%
Gender																		
Locale				4.989	.188	2.9%				6.496	.281	7.9%	4.211	.195	3.0%	5.018	.184	2.9%
	R = .246 R2 = .061 F = 14.47 P<.01			R = .341 R2 = .116 F = 19.5 P<.01			R = .324 R2 = .105 F = 13.1 P < .01			R = .369 R2 = .136 F = 21.90 P < .01			R = .317 R2 = .101 F = 12.499 P < .01			R = .340 R2 = .116 F = 14.57 p<.01		

b = b Coefficient β = β Coefficient Exp. Vari. = Explained Variance

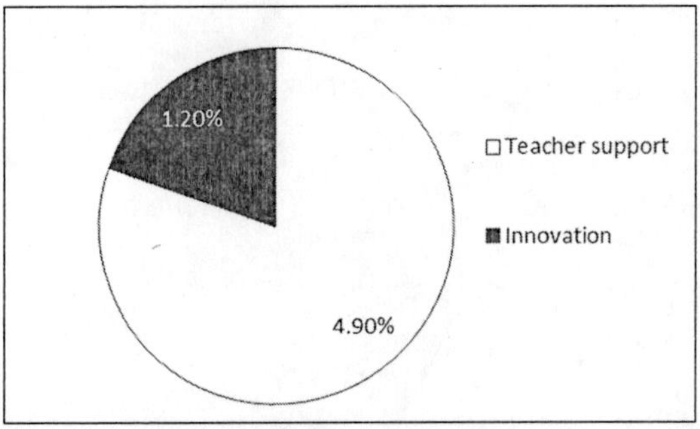

Figure 18(a). Explained variance by significant variable for Hindi subject achievement (Male)

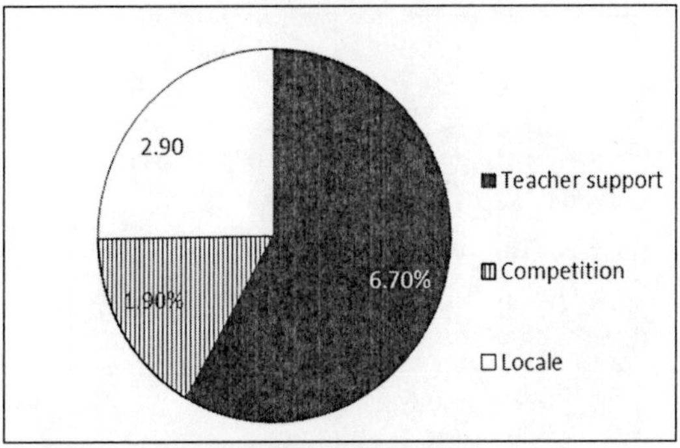

Figure 18(b). Explained variance by significant variable for English subject achievement (Male)

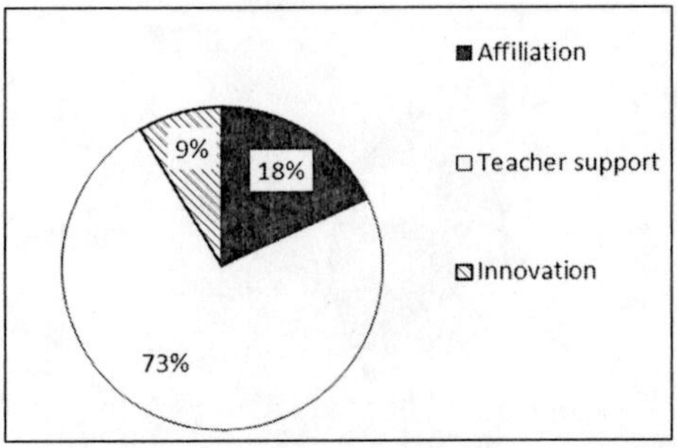

Figure 18(c). Explained variance by significant variable for Sanskrit subject achievement (Male)

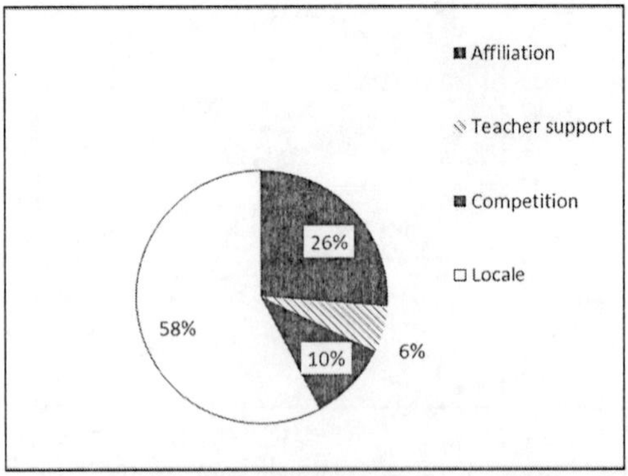

Figure 18(d). Explained variance by significant variable for Mathematics subject achievement (Male)

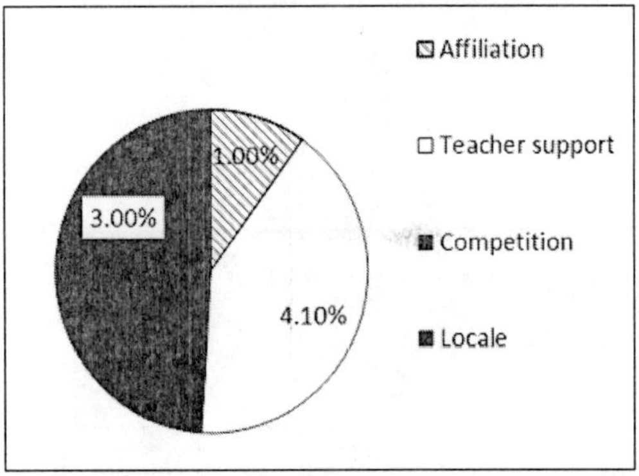

Figure 18(e). Explained variance by significant variable for Science subject achievement (Male)

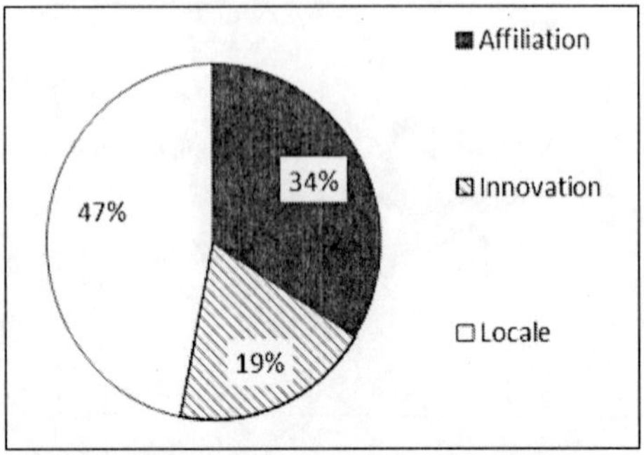

Figure 18(f). Explained variance by significant variable for Social Science subject achievement (Male)

Subject Wise Academic Achievement of Male Students

For male student teacher support was the most important factor and it had emerged out as significant predictor for achievement of all subjects, beta co-efficient shows that It had explained alone 4.9% variance of Hindi achievement, 6.7.0% variance of English achievement, 6.9% variance of Sanskrit achievement, 0.8% variance of math achievement, 4.1% of variance of science achievement and 5.5% variance of social science achievement. Affiliation was the second important factor emerged out as significant predictor for Sanskrit, math, Science and Social Science achievement and explained 1.7% variance of Sanskrit achievement, 3.6% variance of math achievement and 1.0% variance of science achievement and 2.1% variance of social science achievement. Affiliation was the second important variable which play important role for subjects such as Sanskrit, Math Science and Social Science and explained significant variance in these subjects. Competition emerged out as significant predictor for Mathematics, English and science subject and it had explained 1.4% variance of Mathematics achievement, 1.9% variance of English achievement and 1.9% variance of science achievement. Results of the study also supported by Gneeezy, Niederle and Rustichini (2003) in which he found that, as we increase the competitiveness of the environment, a significant increase in performance for men, but not for women. This result shows significant gender gap in performance. Lam, Yim, Law and Cheung (2004) studied the effects of competition on achievement motivation in Chinese classrooms and found that competition had a positive impact on performance goals and learning motivation in the classroom. Result also shows that locale has the significant role for predicting English Math, Science and Social Science achievement of male students and it had explained 2.9% variance of English achievement, 7.9% variance of mathematic achievement, 3.0% variance of science achievement and 2.9% variance of social science achievement. This shows that male students of rural area tend to achieve higher in English, Math, Science and Social Science while trend was opposite for urban male students.

Academic Achievement of Female Students

Results regarding stepwise multiple regression analysis of academic achievement of female students were presented in Table 16 and figure 19.

Table 16. Stepwise multiple regression analysis of academic achievement (Female)

Predictor variable	R	R2	R square change	F change	Unstd. b Coeff.	Std. β Coeff .	t	Explained variance
Constant					143.00		13.5	
Task	.332	.110	.110	61.319	3	..149	44	11%
Orientation	a	.136	.026	14.651	1.354	.153	2.58	2.6%
Affiliation	.369	.147	.011	6.402	1.357	.143	5	1.1%
Innovation	b				1.236		2.69	
	.383c						6	
							2.53	
							0	

$R=.383$, $R^2=.147$ $F=28.304$, $P<.001$

D. V. : Academic achievement

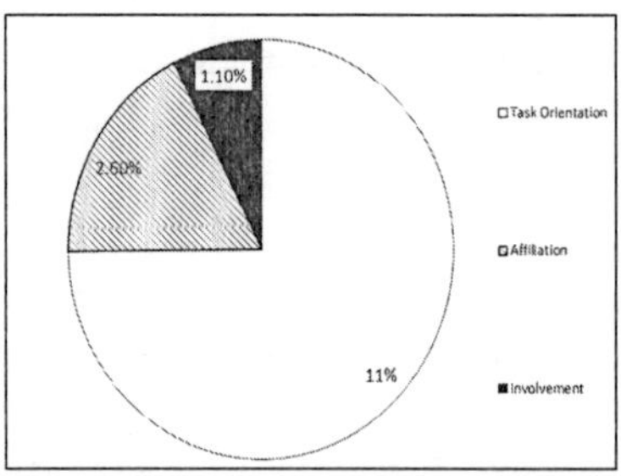

Figure 19: Explained Variance in Academic Achievement of students' by significant variable (Female)

Results of stepwise multiple regression analysis for female students table 16 showed analysis of the data that the multiple co relational co-efficient was found to be .383 which was highly significant (F=28.304, P<.000) its R square was .147. Results regarding Stepwise multiple regression for subject wise achievement of female students are presented in Table 17 and Explained variance in subject wise achievement of students by significant variable are shown in Fig. 19a, 18b, 18c, 18d, 18e, 18f respectively.

Table 17. Stepwise multiple regression for subject wise achievement (Female)

Significant variable	Hindi			English			Sanskrit			Math			Science			Social science		
	b	β	Exp. Vari.	b	β	Exp. Vari.	b	β	Exp. Vari.	b	β	Exp. Vari.	b	β	Exp. Vari.	b	β	Exp. Vari.
(CONSTANT)	20.724			24.474			19.673			19.790			33.433			21.740		
I	.368	.158	10.%				.280	.126	0.9%	.	.							
A				.375	.225	9.8%				.181	.150	1.3%	.272	.209	6.6%	.310	.171	2.1%
TS	.560	.173	2.7%				.448	.145	2.3%							.484	.197	8.3%
TO							.386	.165	10.6%	.182	.147	5.9%						
C																		
O&O																		
RC				.262	.155	1.6%												
TC	.323	.114	1.0%										.156	.101	0.8%			
Inn.																		
Gender																		
Locale	-1.772	- .090	0.8%							.960	.096	0.9%	1.138	.105	1.0%			
	R = .381 R2 = .145 F = 20.842 P<.01			R = .338 R2 = .114 F = 31.706 P<.01			R = .370 R2 = .137 F = 26.091 P < .01			R = .285 R2 = .081 F = 14.562 P < .01			R = .289 R2 = .083 F =14.949 P < .01			R = .322 R2 = .104 F = 28.546 p<.01		

b = b Coefficient β = β Coefficient Exp. Vari. = Explained Variance

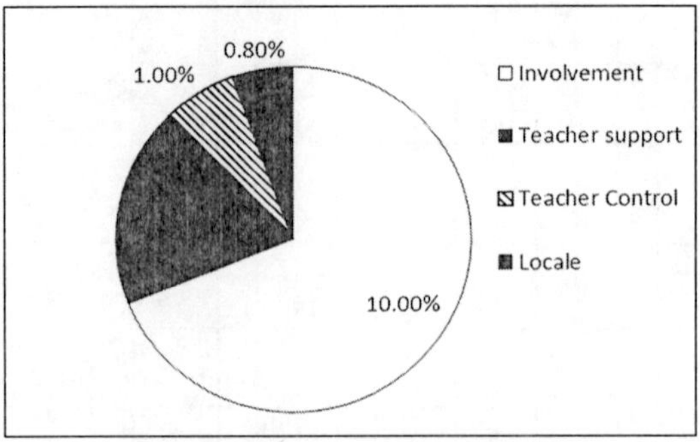

Figure 20(a). Explained variance by significant variable for Hindi subject achievement (Female)

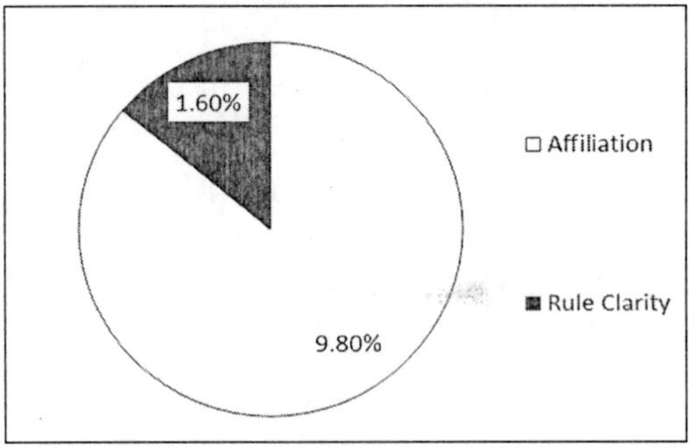

Figure 20(b). Explained variance by significant variable for English subject achievement (Female)

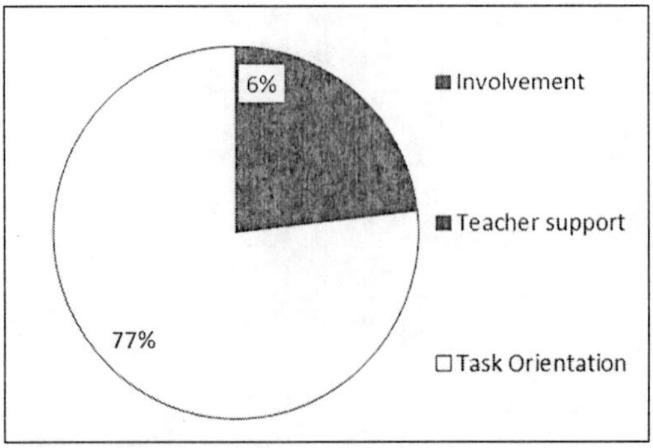

Figure 20(c). Explained variance by significant variable for Sanskrit subject achievement (Female)

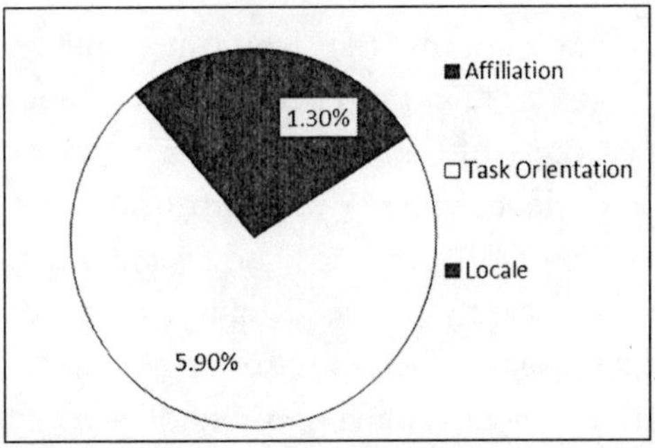

Figure 20(d). Explained variance by significant variable for Mathematics subject achievement (Female)

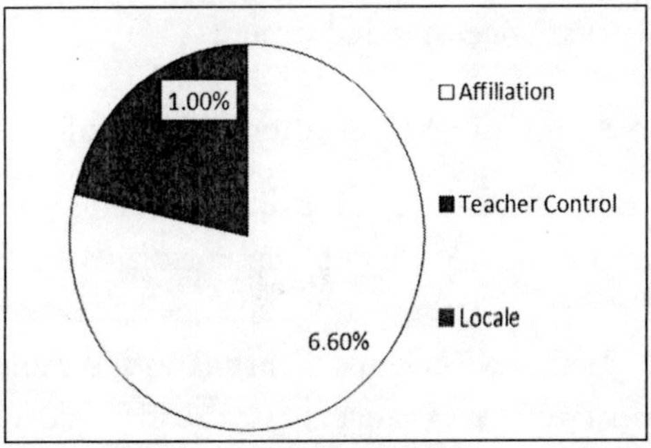

Figure 20(e). Explained variance by significant variable for Science subject achievement (Female)

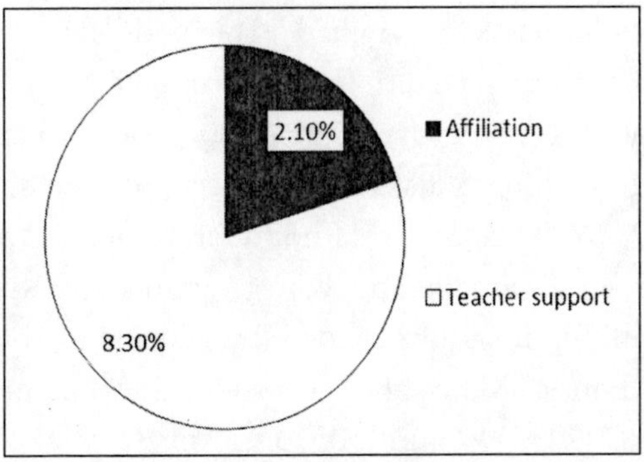

Figure 20(f). Explained variance by significant variable for Social Science subject achievement (Female)

Table 16 indicated that the significant variables included in the present analysis contributed 14.7% variance in the achievement scores of the students. The task orientation, affiliation, and involvement sub-dimension of classroom environment emerge out to be significant predictors contributing significantly in the variation of criterion variable academic achievement. Whereas remaining variables were found to be insignificant in explaining variance of achievement scores of the students. Beta coefficient of significant variables indicated that the task orientation was the most important variables emerged out with a value of .149 and it had explained alone 11.0%of variance of achievement.

Subject Wise Academic Achievement of Female Students

In female students affiliation and Task Orientation dimension were more important. Affiliation dimension was significant for predicting English, Mathematics, science and Social Science achievement. Beta coefficient of affiliation dimension shows that it explained 9.8% variance of English achievement, 1.3% variance of mathematic achievement, 6.6% variance of science achievement and 2.1% variance of social science achievement while task orientation dimension was significant for Sanskrit and Mathematics subjects and it had explained 10.6% variance of Sanskrit achievement and 5.9% variance of Mathematic achievement. Teacher support dimension emerged out significant for Hindi, Sanskrit, and Social Science subject and it explained 2.7% variance of Hindi achievement, 2.3% variance of Sanskrit achievement and 8.3% variance of social science achievement. Findings also shows that locale is the significant factor for Hindi, Math and science, achievement with Beta Coefficient -.099, .096 and .105 respectively, it explained 0.8% variance of Hindi achievement, 0.9% variance of math achievement and 1.0% variance of science achievement. Here the negative nature of beta coefficient for Hindi subject indicated that the achievement of Hindi became less favorable with the increase in ruralness. This shows that ruralness is less favorable for Hindi achievement in female students. Educational statistics have indicated that females are outperforming males at all levels of the school system, attaining more school and post-school qualifications, and attending university in higher numbers (Alton Lee & Praat 2001; House of Representatives Standing Committee on Education and Training, 2002; Mullis *et. al.*, 2003; Office for Standards in Education, 2003). A gap between the achievement of boys and girls has been found, with girls showing better performance than boys in certain instances (Chambers & Schreiber, 2004). Previous research has shown that student gender is a significant predictor of classroom environment perceptions. A consistent pattern of girls perceiving the classroom environment more positively than boys is evident (e.g. Fraser & Chionh, 2000; Lawrenz, 1987). Two relatively recent studies on the effect of gender confirm this view. Fisher, den Brok, and Rickards's (2006), Koul and Fisher (2006). Research on gender differences in classroom environment perceptions was also conducted in various countries (Fisher, Fraser & Rickards, 1997; Fisher, Rickards, Goh, & Wong, 1997; Fraser, Giddings & Mc Robbie, 1995; Henderson, Fisher & Fraser, 2000; Wong & Fraser, 1997). Owens and Straton (1980) found that girls preferred cooperation more than boys but boys preferred competition and individualization more than girls. Overall, these studies have shown that girls generally hold more favorable perceptions of their classroom learning environments than boys in the same classes

Thus we find that the hypothesis stating that sex has the significant role to determine academic achievement of the students was accepted only for urban area and rejected for rural area.

From the above discussion it may be concluded that classroom environment was found positively related to students academic achievement. Since it shows that there was a positive correlation, it can be concluded that the more conducive classroom environment as perceived by the students, the better their academic achievement would be. Affiliation, teacher support and teacher control were the most important dimension of classroom environment which emerged out as significant predictor for academic achievement of the students of Chhattisgarh. For subject wise achievement teacher support and affiliation dimension were emerged out significant predictor for all subjects i.e. Hindi, English, Mathematics, Science, Social Science whereas teacher control dimension was emerged out as significant predictor for Math, Science and Social Science subjects., Role of Locale was also proved to significantly influence academic achievement of the students. Role of femininity was found to significant only for urban area.

6

Summary

INTRODUCTION

Measuring achievement is a major part of the learning process and informs educators of student talent and progress toward educational goals. Today's modern society expects each one to be a high achiever. It has become an indicator of a child's future. The world is rapidly changing and the "modern society expects everyone to be a high achiever" (Daulta, 2008). However, "success in any meaningful endeavor is marked by a history of high expectations that provide the challenge and inspiration necessary to press the individual to his/her highest level of performance" (Ozturk & Debelak, 2005) and no matter what the obstacles are, everyone is encouraged to succeed because those who succeed are valued and considered important by society members.

According to Steinberger (1993) "Academic achievement generally refers to the level of success attained in some specific or general area concerning scholastic or academic work. Achievement encompasses the student's ability and performance. It is a multidimensional and it is intricately related to human growth and cognitive, emotional, social and physical development, it reflects the whole child; it is not related to a single instance, but occurs across time and levels, through a student's life in public school and on into post-secondary years and working life". Academic achievement is a component of the wider term educational growth. It is unique, prime and perennial responsibility of an educational institution established by a society to promote a wholesome academic growth and development of the child. Achievement means the extent to which learner is profiting from instructions in a given area of learning. It is the outcome of general and specific learning experience. In other words, academic achievement may be defined as the competence students actually show in school subjects in whom they have received instruction (Sing, 2012). The world is becoming more and more competitive; quality of performance has become the key factor for personal progress. Parents desire that their children climb the ladder of performance to as high a level as possible. This desire for a high level of achievement puts a lot of pressure on students, teachers and schools and in general the education system itself. In fact, it appears as if the whole system of education revolves round the academic achievement of students, though various other outcomes are also expected from the system thus a lot of time and effort of the schools are used for helping students to achieve better in their scholastic endeavors. The importance of scholastic and academic achievement has raised important questions for educational researchers. What factors promote achievement in students? How far do the different factors contribute towards academic achievement (Ramaswamy, 1990).

Factors affecting academic achievement of the students can be grouped into three main categories i.e., personal or individual factor, school factor and socio cultural factor. Personal factor includes intelligence, motivation, self-concept, study habit, anxiety, interest, level of aspiration, as the determinants of academic achievement, among which intelligence, motivation, study habit and anxiety acquire relevance, school factor includes all the variables directly connected with school i.e. school environment and classroom environment, teacher education, student teacher relationship, teaching method etc. In the present study classroom environment and its various dimensions were taken as predictor of academic achievement. Socio-cultural factors include socio economic status, educational level of parents, income of the family, occupation of the father, occupation of the mother etc. Keeping in view the all factors that affect student's academic achievement, the present study emphasise on classroom environment as a correlates of academic achievement.

Classroom environment has become an important area for educational research because most learning takes place there. The importance of the classroom learning environment has been increasingly recognized internationally over the past 50 years. According to Wilson (1996) classroom learning environment is a place where learners and teachers interact with each other and use a variety of tools and information resources in their pursuit of learning activities. Research in education that focuses on classroom and school-level learning environments has produced promising findings leading to an enhancement of the teaching and learning process Classroom environment is seen as a major determiner of classroom behavior and learning, understanding how to establish and maintain a positive classroom climate is seen as basic to improving schools. The classroom is the basic unit of organization of the educational system. By continuing to increase the knowledge of the interactions that occur within the classroom, the quality of education can be improved with understanding of students development, and their perception about learning environment.

Classroom environment encompasses a broad range of educational concepts, including the physical setting, the psychological environment created through social contexts, and numerous instructional components related to teacher characteristics and behaviors. How can we organize the environment in the school and classroom so that such interactions support and enhance both teaching and learning, and where children feel safe, happy and wanted, and which teachers find meaningful and professionally satisfying? Yet not enough attention is paid to the importance of classroom environment for learning. Often classrooms are overcrowded, with no alternative spaces to learn, nor are they attractive, inviting or sensitive towards children's needs. The learning environment has a big influence on student outcomes and plays an important role in improving the efficiency of learning in all levels of classrooms. Studies consistently have shown evidence of relations between student perceptions of their classroom learning environment and their cognitive and affective outcomes. Students learn better when they perceive their classroom environment positively. Keeping in view the importance of classroom environment in relation to academic achievement of the rural and urban students. The present study aimed to investigate the relationship between classroom environment along with its various sub dimensions, locale and sex with academic achievement. The literature review clearly indicates that there is a greater need for emphasis on the classroom environment that may enhance academic achievement of students

Problems and Hypotheses

The first problem of the study was to investigate the relationship of academic achievement to classroom environment along with its various sub dimensions i.e., involvement, affiliation, teacher support, task orientation, competition, order and organization, rule clarity, teacher control and innovation. It was hypothesized that classroom environment (along with its various dimensions i.e. involvement, affiliation teacher support, task orientation, competition, order and organization, rule clarity, teacher control and innovation,) would contribute significantly to academic achievement of the student.

The second problem of the study was to see the role of locale to determine the academic achievement of the student in relation to various sub dimensions of classroom environment. It was hypothesized that locale would predict significantly to academic achievement of the student in relation to various dimensions of classroom environment namely, involvement, affiliation teacher support, task orientation, competition, order and organization, rule clarity, teacher control and innovation.

Another problem of the present study was to see the role of sex to determine academic achievement of the students in relation to various dimensions of classroom environment namely involvement, affiliation teacher support, task orientation, competition, order and organization, rule clarity, teacher control and innovation. It was hypothesized that sex would predict significantly to academic achievement of the student in relation to various dimensions of classroom environment.

Sample

Initially a larger number of students studying class X of different Higher Secondary State Government Schools of Chhattisgarh region were randomly selected, out of which 941 subjects were retained as final sample. In the present study the sample were selected from two different locales i.e. rural and urban. The age range of the subjects was 15-17 years.

Measures

Classroom Environment Scale

To assess classroom environment, classroom environment scale CES constructed and standardized by Moos and Trickett (1974), adaptation and standardization to suit the Indian conditions in Hindi Joshi and Vyas (1987) was used. CES scale has four dimensions comprising of nine subscales which reflect a conceptualization of the relationships among them. The four Dimensions and the nine sub-dimensions are as follows:

Relationship Dimension

Measures the extent to which students have attentive interest in class activities and participated in discussion do additional work on their own and enjoy the class is considered. The nature and intensity of personal relationship within the environment and the extent to which people are involved in the environment and support one another. This dimension includes Involvement, Affiliation, and Teacher support sub dimensions.

(i) Involvement (I): Involvement measures the extent to which student have attentive interest in the class activities and participate in discussion. The extent to which students do additional work on their own and enjoy the class is considered.

(ii) Affiliation (A): Affiliation assesses the level of friendship student feel for each other i.e., the extent to which they help each other with homework, get to know each other easily and working together.

(iii) Teacher Support (TS): Teacher Support measures the amount of help, concern and friendship the teacher directs toward the students.

Personal Development

The basic direction along which personal growth and self-enhancement tend to occur. Factors such as Task orientation and Competition were included in this dimension.

(i) Task Orientation (TO): measure the extent to which it is important to complete the activities that have been planned.

(ii) Competition (C): Competition assesses the emphasis placed on student competing with each other for grades recognition.

System Maintenance

The extent, to which the environment is orderly, clear in expectation, maintains control and is responsive to change. This dimension included factors such as order and organization, rule clarity and teacher control.

(i) Order and Organization (O&O): Order & Organization Assesses the emphasis on students behaving in an orderly and polite manner and on the overall organization of assignment and classroom activities. The degree to which students tend to remain calm and quite is considered.

(ii) Rule Clarity (RC): Assess the emphasis on establishing and following a clear set of rules and on students knowing what the consequences will be the extent to which the teacher is consistent in dealing with students who break rules.

(iii) Teacher control (TC): Measure how strict the teacher is in enforcing the rules and the severity of the punishment for rule infractions. The number of rules and the ease of students getting in trouble are considered.

System Change Dimension

(i) Innovation (Inn): Innovation measures how much student contributes to planning classroom activities and the amount of unusual and varying activities and assignments planned by the teacher. The extent to which the teacher attempts to use new technique and encourage creative thinking in the students is considered.

Classroom environment scale consist of 78 items which cover the almost all the important constitutes of its main dimension, i. e. Involvement, Affiliation, Teacher Support, Task Orientation, Competition, Order and Organization, Rule Clarity, Teacher Control and Innovation.

To assess academic achievement of the student, overall marks and marks obtained by the student in different subjects, viz- Hindi, English, Mathematics, Science, and Social Science in class 10th annual examination was used.

Design

The present study is co relational research employing type-s independent variable the main objective of the study is to find out relationship of academic achievement with classroom environment along with its various sub dimensions, locale and sex. The predictors undertaken in the study are classroom environment along with its nine sub dimensions (i.e. involvement, affiliation, teacher support, task orientation, competition, order organization, rule clarity, teacher control and innovation), locale and sex. The criterion variable is academic achievement of the student. To fulfill the above mentioned objective Pearsons product moment coefficient of correlation and stepwise multiple regression analysis technique was applied.

Procedure

After explaining the objectives of the research work permission was obtained from the principles of the selected schools to administer the questionnaires to the students of tenth standard. To establish a good rapport with the subject it was assured that their responses and identities would be strictly kept confidential and not disclose anywhere, Thus they were made independent to give their answer comfortably and honestly, whatever they felt. In this way subjects were encouraged to give their proper cooperation during the testing.

The classroom environment scale booklets were distributed to the subjects. The printed instructions were explained to the subjects. The subjects were seated in group settings. A response sheet was provided with each booklet for the subjects to mark their responses. The classroom where the test was administered was well organized and the seating arrangement was also made comfortable. After the completion of test booklets were also collected back .The participant students, principal and the staffs of the school were given thanks for their cooperation.

After having administered the test as per procedure laid down and collection of the answer sheets and booklets is to be completed. It must be noted that each item of every scale is on a five point scale of "4 to 0", There are some negatively framed items for which the scoring is in reverse direction of scoring weightage, i.e. "0 to 4".The total score of each sub scale has to be obtained by adding score obtained on each respective items of that scale. Thus, for each sub scale total score is obtained and interpreted.

After scoring, the data was organized and put for the statistical analysis. The data was analyzed with the help of appropriate statistical techniques, in order to verify the formulated hypotheses.

RESULTS AND DISCUSSION

The findings of the present study showed that students academic achievement results were related in a positive direction with all sub scales of classroom environment namely, involvement, affiliation teacher support, task orientation, competition, order organization, rule clarity, teacher control and innovation. Results showed that among correlated variables to academic achievement affiliation has the highest correlation (r=.282) with academic achievement, after this task orientation, involvement rule clarity, teacher control, competition, order and organization, teacher support, and locale (ruralness) were respectively have significant positive correlation to academic achievement.

Results of stepwise multiple regression analysis for academic achievement showed that the model of regression analysis is significant, as the R square =.108 F= 28.401, p < .01 indicates the strength of model. It is observed that 10.8% variance of i.e. taken in total is contributed significantly in the variation of the criterion variable academic achievement. Affiliation, task orientation, teacher control dimension of classroom environment and locale emerged out to be significant predictors contributing significantly in the variation of criterion variable academic achievement whereas the other remaining variables i.e involvement, teacher support, competition, order and organization, rule clarity and innovation were found to be insignificant in explaining variance of academic achievement . The beta coefficient of significant variables indicated that the affiliation dimension of classroom environment was the most important variable emerged out and explained alone 7.9% variation in student's academic achievement. Affiliation assesses the level of friendship student feel for each other i.e. the extent to which they help each other with homework, get to know each other easily and working together. Task orientation was second significant variable with beta coefficient value .118 and it had explained 1.5% variation in the criterion variable. Task Orientation measure the extent to which it is important to complete the activities that have been planned.

The second problem of the study is to see the role of locale in academic achievement in relation to various dimensions of classroom environment. Results of multiple regression analysis showed that locale play significant role in determining the academic achievement, to find out the best predictors in rural area for academic achievement of the students the model of regression analysis for academic achievement of rural students was found to be significant as the R = .386, R Square = .149, F = 32.279, P < .000 which indicated significant strength of the model. Model shows that the significant variables included in the present analysis contributed to 14.9% of variance in determining the academic achievement of the rural students. Affiliation, task orientation and competition, dimension of classroom environment emerged out to be the significant predictors contributing significantly in the variation of criterion variable. In urban area students Model of regression analysis was found to significant with (R = .301, R = 091) (F = 12.786, p < .01) R square.091 which indicated that significant variables included in the present analysis contributed to 9.1% of variance in determining the achievement of the students. In urban area involvement, teacher control sub dimension of classroom environment and sex emerged out to be significant predictors contributing significantly in the variation of criterion variable.

Another problem of the present study was to see the role of sex in academic achievement. Results of multiple regression analysis showed that sex play significant role to determine academic achievement in urban area, to find out the best predictors in male and female students for academic achievement. The separate stepwise multiple regression analysis for academic achievement of male and female students was carried out. For male students, analysis of the data reveal that the multiple co relational co-efficient was found to be .361 which was highly significant (F = 16.73, P < .01) its R square was .130, which indicated that the significant variables included in the present analysis contributed 13.9% variance in the achievement scores of the students. Teacher support, affiliation, competition dimension of classroom environment and locale emerged out to be significant predictors contributing significantly in the variation of criterion variable, i.e., academic achievement. Whereas remaining variables were found to be insignificant in explaining variance of achievement scores of male and female students.

For the female students, analysis of the data shows that the multiple co relational co-efficient was found to be .383 which was highly significant ($F = 28.304$, $P < .01$) its R square was .147, which indicated that the significant variables included in the present analysis contributed 14.7% variance in the achievement scores of the students. The task orientation, affiliation, and involvement dimension of classroom environment emerge out to be the significant predictors contributing significantly in the variation of criterion variable academic achievement. Whereas remaining variables were found to be insignificant in explaining variance of achievement scores of the students. Beta coefficient of significant variables indicated that the task orientation was the most important variables emerged out with a value of .149 and it had explained alone 11.0% of variance of achievement.

Results Regarding Subject wise Achievement in Relation to Classroom Environment, Locale and Sex

To investigate the role of different dimensions of classroom environment for subject wise achievement of the students, subject wise regression analysis was carried out. Findings revealed that in Chhattisgarh Region teacher support emerged out as the most significant factor for achievement of all subjects. Results also showed that teacher control dimension was important for Mathematics, Science and Social Science achievements. Role of sex was found to be significant for Hindi and Sanskrit subjects while role of locale was found to be significant for English, Math, Science and Social Science subjects. It showed that in government schools of Chhattisgarh achievement of Hindi and Sanskrit subjects increases with femininity and achievement of English, Mathematics, Science and Social Science was more associated with locale/ruralness.

Results showed that in rural area teacher support was the most important factor emerged out as significant predictor for predicting subject wise achievements. Affiliation was the second important factor emerged out as significant predictor for English, Sanskrit, Science and Social Science achievement. Competition dimension was found to be significant predictor for Mathematics and English achievement. Result also indicates that for Mathematics subject femininity plays the negative role.

For male student teacher support was the most important factor and it had emerged out as significant predictor for subject wise achievement. Affiliation was the second important variable which play important role for subjects such as Sanskrit, Mathematics Science and Social Science and explained significant variance in these subjects. Competition emerged out as significant predictor for Mathematics, English and science subject. Result also shows that locale has the significant role for predicting English Mathematics, Science and Social Science achievement of male students. This shows that male students of rural area tend to achieve higher in English, Mathematics, Science and Social Science while this trend was opposite for urban male students. In female student's affiliation and Task Orientation dimension were more important. Affiliation dimension was significant for predicting English, Maths, Science and Social Science achievement while task orientation dimension was significant for Sanskrit and math subjects.

CONCLUSION

The purpose of the present study was to examine the role of classroom environment along with its various dimensions, locale and sex on academic achievement of the students. The findings of correlation showed that there is a statistically significant positive correlation with all dimensions of classroom environment namely involvement, affiliation teacher support, task orientation, competition, order and organization, rule clarity, teacher control and innovation. Findings of stepwise multiple regression analysis pointed out that in Chhattisgarh region teacher support, affiliation, task orientation, teacher control and locale.

The following conclusions were drawn from the study regarding academic achievement in relation to classroom environment, locale and sex.

Conclusions Regarding Overall Academic Achievement

- Academic achievement of the student increased with increase in affiliation.
- Academic achievement of the student increased with increase in task orientation.
- Academic achievement of the student increased with increase in teacher control.
- Academic achievement of the student increased in the subjects being from rural area.

Conclusions Regarding Subject Wise Academic Achievement

- Academic achievement of all subjects i.e. Hindi, English, Sanskrit, Mathematics, Science and Social Science increases with increase in Affiliation.

- Academic achievement of all subjects i.e. Hindi, English, Sanskrit, Mathematics, Science and Social Science increases with increase in Teacher Support.
- Academic achievement of Hindi, Mathematics, Science and Social Science increased with increases in teacher control.
- Academic achievement of Sanskrit increased with increases in teacher support and task orientation.
- Academic achievement of Hindi and Sanskrit increased with increases in femininity.
- Academic achievement of English, Mathematics, Science and social science increases with increase in ruralness.

Conclusions Regarding Overall Academic Achievement of Rural Students

- Academic achievement of the student increased with increase in affiliation.
- Academic achievement of the student increased with increases in task orientation.
- Academic achievement of the student increased with increases in competition.

Conclusions Regarding Subject Wise Achievement of Rural Students

- Academic achievement of all subjects i.e. Hindi, English, Sanskrit, Mathematics, Science and Social Science increased with increase in teacher support.

- Academic achievement of all subjects i.e. English, Sanskrit, Science and Social Science increased with increase in affiliation.
- Academic achievement of English, and Mathematics increased with increases in competition.
- Academic achievement of Mathematics decreased with increase in femininity.

Conclusions Regarding Overall Academic Achievement of Urban Student

- Academic achievement of the student increased with increases in involvement.
- Academic achievement of the student increased with increases in teacher control.
- Academic achievement of the student increased in the subjects being females.

Conclusions Regarding Subject Wise Achievement of Urban Students

- Academic achievement of Hindi, English, Sanskrit and Social Science increased with increases in involvement.
- Academic achievement of Hindi, English, Mathematics, Science and Social. Science increased with increases in teacher control.
- Academic achievement of Hindi increased with increases in femininity.
- Academic achievement of Mathematics increased with increases in affiliation.

Conclusions Regarding Overall Academic Achievement of Male Students

- Academic achievement of the student increased with increases in teacher support.
- Academic achievement of the student increased in the subjects being from rural area.
- Academic achievement of the student increased with increases in affiliation.
- Academic achievement of the student increased with increases in competition.

Conclusions Regarding Subject Wise Academic Achievement of Male Students

- Academic achievement of all subjects i.e. Hindi, English, Sanskrit, Mathematics, Science and Social Science increased with increase in Teacher Support.
- Academic achievement of Sanskrit, Mathematics, Science and Social Science increased with increase in affiliation.
- Academic achievement, English, Mathematics, Science and Social Science increased with increase in competition.

Conclusion Regarding Overall Academic Achievement of Female Students

- Academic achievement of the student increased with increases in task orientation.
- Academic achievement of the student increased with increases in affiliation.

- Academic achievement of the student increased with increases in involvement.

Conclusion regarding Subject Wise Academic Achievement of female students

- Academic achievement of English, Mathematics, Science and Social Science increased with increases in affiliation.
- Academic achievement of Sanskrit and Mathematics increased with increases in task orientation.
- Academic achievement of Hindi increased with increases in involvement.

IMPLICATIONS AND SUGGESTIONS

Findings of this study may have implications in educational sector. From the above findings it may be said that teachers and educational administrators may benefit from an increased awareness of the classroom psychosocial environment. Teacher support, affiliation, task orientation and involvement factors may increase the academic achievement of the students. In sum, these findings could provide useful information for those who wish to develop educational programs to improve students' academic achievement.

The study was confined only to Chhattisgarh state, so it cannot be claimed to have comprehensiveness. It is therefore suggested that study may be conducted on other states also to establish the results rationally.

The study was conducted only on class tenth students of the Government schools. It may be conducted on students of Private schools, Technical Institutions and University.

The present study was confined to classroom environment as correlates of academic achievement, more psychosocial correlates should be considered.

Further research is needed to determine relationship between the actual and the preferred classroom climate by the students in addition to quantitative methods, qualitative approaches should be implemented to determine classroom environment perceptions. This study may have been more extensive if both quantitative and qualitative measures of climate had been incorporated.

Bibliography

Abu-Hilal & Maher, M. (2000). A structural model of attitudes towards school subjects, academic aspiration and achievement. *Educational Psychology*, 20(1), 75-84.

Adeyemo, D. A. (2005). Parental Involvement, Interest in Schooling and School Environment as predictors of academic self-efficacy among fresh secondary school students in Oyo State, Nigeria. *Electronic Journal of Psychology of Education* 5 (3): 1-15

Aguele, L. I. & Agwugah, N. V. (2007). Female Participation in Science, Technology and Mathematics (STM) Education in Nigeria and National Development. *Journal of Social Science, 15 (2),* 121-126.

Ahmad, A., Hamid, M. M., & Ganaie, M. Y. (2012) Self-concept, level of aspiration and academic achievement of physically challenged and normal students at secondary level in district Barramullah, *IISTE, Research on Humanities and Social Sciences,2 (2)*

Akhter, S. (2003). The relationships between teachers' control orientations perceived teachers' control behavior and students motivation, Ph.D. Thesis, Macquarie University, Sydney, Australia.

Aldridge, J. M. Fraser, B. J. (2001). A cross-cultural study of classroom learning environments in Australia and Taiwan. *Learning Environments Research*, 3, 101–134

Allik, J. & Realo, A (2006) "Intelligence, Academic Abilities and Personality", *Personality and Individual Differences,* Vol.23, No. 5, retrieved from, http://www.sciencedirect.com1997,accessed on February, pp 809-814.

Allport, G.W. (1961). *Pattern and Growth in Personality.* New York: Holt, Rinehart, & Winston.

Alokan, F. B. & Arijesuyo, A. E. (2013) Rural and Urban Differential in Student's Academic Performance among Secondary School Students In Ondo State, Nigeria, *Journal of Educational and Social Research*, 3(3),213-217

Al-qaisy, L. M. (2011). The relation of depression and anxiety in academic achievement among group of university students, *International Journal of Psychology and Counselling.* Vol. 3 (5), 96-100.

Alton-Lee, A., & Praat, A. (2001). Explaining and addressing gender differences in the New Zealand compulsory school sector. Wellington: Ministry of Education.

Ames, C. (1987). "The Enhancement of Student Motivation." In *Advances in Motivation and Achievement*, Vol 5: Enhancing Motivation, edited by Martin L. Maehr and Douglas A. Kleiber. 123-148. Greenwich, Connecticut: Academic Press.

.... (1992). Classrooms: Goals, structures and student motivation. *Journal of Educational Psychology, 84*(3), 262-271.

Anand, C. L., & Padma, M. S., (1987). Correlates of achievement. In M.B. Buch, Ed. (1987), *Third survey of research in education*, Baroda: SERD, 648.

Anderman, L. H., & Midgley, C. (1997). Motivation and middle school students. In J. L. Irvin (Ed.), *what current research says to the middle level practitioner* (pp. 41-48). Columbus, OH: National Middle School Association.

Anderson, C. S. (1982). The search for school climate: A review of the research. *Review of Educational Research*, 52, 3, pp. 368-420.

Anderson, G., & Walberg, H. (1974). Evaluating educational performance. In H. J. Walberg (Ed.), *Evaluating educational performance: A sourcebook of methods, instruments, and examples* (pp. 81-98). Berkley, CA: Mc Cutchan.

Arias, M. B. (1986). The context of education for Hispanic Students: an overview. *American Journal of Education,* (26-57).

Arigbabu, A. A. & Mji, A. (2004). Is Gender a Factor in Mathematics Performance among Nigerian Preservice Teachers? *Sex Role, 51 (11* & *12)*, 749.

Arisoy, N. (2007). Examining 8th Grade students perception of learning environment of science classroom in relation to motivational beliefs and attitudes, Thesis, Middle East Technical University.

Astin, A. W. (1984). Student involvement: A developmental theory for higher education. *Journal of College Student Development, 40*(5), 518-529.

.... (1993). *What matters in college: Four critical years revisited.* San Francisco: Jossey-Bass.

Astone, N. M. & Mc Lanahan, S. S. (1991). Family structure, parental practices and high school completion. *American Sociological Review*, 56(3), 309-320

Australian Education Council. (1989). The Common and Agreed National Goal of Schooling. Canberra: AGPS Brookover, W.B. and Lezotte, L.A. (1979). Changes in schools characteristics co incident with changes in student achievement. East Learning, MI: Michigan State University.

Ayodele, C. S. & Adebiyi, D. R. (2013). Study habits influence of academic performance of university under-graduates in Nigeria, *Research Journal in Organizational Psychology and Educational Studies,* 2 (3), 72-75.

Baek, S. G. & Choi, H. J. (2002) The relationship between students perceptions of classroom environment and their academic achievement in Korea, *Asia Pacific Education Review 3(1):125-135.*

Baker, J. A. (1999), Teacher student interaction in urban at risk classrooms: differential behavior relationship quality and student satisfaction with school. *Elementary school Journal,* 100, 57-70.

Balusubramanian, P. S. (1997) Correlates of achievement. In NCERT (1997), *Fifth Survey of Educational Research,* New Delhi: NCERT, 723-735.

Bamman, S. S., and Ksheersagar S. S., (2008) Self Concept and Academic Achievement among Students. *Indian Journal of Psychometry and Education,* 38,(.1), 57-59.

Bank, C. & Finlapson, W. (1980). *Successful Motivation of Students in Academic Activities* in McClelland, D. C. Appleton-Century-Crafts.

Banta, T. (2001) Learning communities illustrate principle of good practice. Assessment update, 13(4), Retrieved June 15, 2004, from academic search premier.

Bartholomy, A. C (1996), Students and teachers as partners in the classroom community: A study of classroom social environment. *VCCA Jounal,* 10, (1), 32-38.

Battistich, V., & Hom, A. (1997). The relationship between students sense of their school as a community and their involvement in problem behaviors. *American Journal of Public Health,* 87, 1997–2001.

Battistich, V., Solomon, D., Kim, D., Watson, M., & Schaps, E. (1995). Schools as communities, poverty levels of student populations, and students attitudes, motives, and performance: A multilevel analysis. *American Educational Research Journal,* 32, 627– 658

Benbow, C. P., & Stanley, J. C. (1980). Sex differences in mathematical ability: fact or artifact? *Science,* 210 (4475), 1262-1264.

Bennett, J. (2001). The relationship between classroom climate and student achievement, Ph.D. Thesis, Educational administration, University of North Texas.

Bennett, N. (1976). Teaching Styles and Pupil Progress. London: Open Books.

Berndt, T. J. (1999). Friends' influence on children's adjustment to school relationships as developmental context, *The Minnesota Symposia on Child Psychology,* 30. 85-108, Mahwah, NJ: Erlbaum.

Betty, T., (2004) *Best Practices School Climate and Learning,* .31, MSU, 1-10.

Bilesanmi-Awoderu, J. B. (2006). Effect of Computer-assisted Instruction and Simulation/Games on the Academic Achievement of Secondary School Students in Biology. *Sokoto Educational Review, 8 (1),* 49-60.

Billings, D. (2000). Women's Way of Knowing and the Digital Divide. Presented in an Interactive Paper Presentation.

Binay, P., (2014) My School is RTE compliant! "some key indicators for every school!http://www.academia.edu/4777588/

Birch, S. H., & Ladd, G. W. (1997). The teacher-child relationship and children's early school adjustment. *Journal of School Psychology, 35,* 61–79.

Blackwell, D. L. & McLaughlin, D. K., (1999). Do rural youth attain their educational goals? *Rural Development Perspectives* 13(3), 37-44.

Bolender, M. (1997). A study of the evolving image of a new school within the context of school effectiveness (online) available http://www.ssta.sk.ca/research/school improvement/97-08. htm.

Boylan, C., & Mcswan, D. (1978): Long Staying Rural Teachers who are to blame? Australion *Journal of Education,* 42 (1), 213-223.

Brand, S., Felner, R., Shim, M., Seitsinger, A., & Dumas, T. (2003). Middle school improvement and reform: Development and validation of a school-level assessment of climate, cultural pluralism, and school safety. *Journal of Educational Psychology*, 95, 570 –588

Brophy, J., (1987). "Socializing Students to Learn." In *Advances in Motivation and Achievement,* Vol 5: Enhancing Motivation, edited by Martin L. Maehr and Douglas A. Kleiber. 181-210.Greenwich, Connecticut: Academic Press, 335

Buch, M. B., (1974). *A survey of research in education,* Baroda: Case.

Burnett, P. C. (2002) Teacher praise and feedback and students perceptions of the classroom environment. *Educational Psychology*, 22(1), 5-16.

Byrne, B. & Shavelson, R. (1996) On the structure of self-concept for pre early and late adolescent; A test of the Shavelson, hubner and Stanton(1976) model, *Journal of Personality and Social Psychology,* 70, 599-613.

Campbell, J., Hombo, C., & Mazzeo, J. (1999). NAEP 1999 trends in academic progress: Three decades of student performance. *Education Statistics Quarterly*, 2, 4.

Carrol, J. B., (1993*) Human Cognitive Ability: A survey of factor analysis studies.* Cambridge: Cambridge University Press.

Casanova, P. F. Torre, M. J. De. la, & Carpio, M. de la Villa (2005) Influence of family and socio-demographic variables on students with low academic achievement *Educational Psychology*; 25(4):423-435.

Cassady, J. C. & Johnson, R. E. (2002). Cognitive text anxiety and academic performance. *Contemporary Educational Psychology*, 27 (270-295).

Ceballo, R., McLoyd, V., & Toyokawa, T. (2004). The influence of neighborhood quality on adolescents' educational values and school efforts. *Journal of Adolescent Research*, 19 (6), 716-739

Chambers, E. A., & Schreiber, J. B. (2004). Girls' academic achievement: Varying associations of extracurricular activities. *Gender and Education, 16*(3), 327-346.

Chang, C. Y. Hsiao, C. H. & Barufaldi, J. P. (2006). Preferred–actual learning environment "spaces" and earth science outcomes in Taiwan. *Science. Education*, 90 (3) 420–433.

Cheng, Y. C. (1994). Classroom environment and student affective performance: An effective profile. *Journal of Experimental Education, 62 (3),* 221-240.

Chepell, M. S. *et. al.* (2005). Text anxiety and academic performance in under-graduate and graduate students. *Journal of Educational Psychology*, 97(2), 268-274.

Chiaki Konishi, Shelley Hymel, Bruno D. Zumbo, & Zhen Li. (2010). Do school bullying and Student–Teacher relationships matter for academic achievement? A multilevel analysis. *Canadian Journal of School Psychology, 25*(1).

Chinoh, Y. H., & Fraser, B. J., (1998). Validation of the 'what is happening in this class' Rhostienaire. Paper presented at the annual meeting of the National Association for Research in Science Teaching, San Diego, CA.

Chiu, L. H., & Tulley, M. (1997). Student preferences of teacher discipline styles. *Journal of Instructional Psychology, 24*(3), 168–175.

Chrispeels, J., (1992) Using an effective schools framework to build home-school partnerships for student success. Occasional paper prepared for the National Centre for Effective Schools Wisconsin, Centre for Education Research, University of Wisconsin-Madison

Coakley, J. (1994). *Sport in society: Issues and controversies* (4th ed.). St. Louis: Times Mirror/Mosbey College.

Coleman, J., Campbell, E., Hobson, C., McParland, J., Mood, A., Weinfield, F., & York, R. (1966). *Equality of educational opportunity.* Washington, D.C.: U.S. Government Printing Office.

Colom, R. & Mendoza, E. F. C., (2006) Intelligence Predicts Scholastic Achievement Irrespective of SES Factors, Evidence from Brazil, University of Madrid, Spain, *Intelligence,* 35,(3), 243-251

Combs, A., & Snygg, D. (1959). *Individual behavior: A Perceptual Approach.* (Revised ed.) New York: Harpers.

Cornell, D., & Grossberg, I. (1987). Family environment and personality adjustment in gifted program children. *Gifted Child Quarterly*, 31(2), 59-64.

Cornell, J. P. & Wellborn, J. G. (1991). Competence autonomy and relatedness: A motivational analysis of self system process. In M. Cunnar and

Sroufe (Ed.) Minnesota Symposium on Child Psychology (22) Hillsdale. NJ: Erlbaum.

Crow, L. D., & Crow, A. (1969). *Adolescent development and adjustment.* United States: Mc Graw-Hill.

Crowyn, R. F., & Bradley, R. F. (2002). *Family process mediators of the relation between SES and child outcomes.* Unpublished manuscript, University of Arkansas at Little Rock.

Croxford, L. (2000) *Gender and National Curricular: Shifting Agendas in the UK and Europe.* London: Routledge. http://www.ero.govt.nz/publications /pubs2000/ promoting % 20boys % 20achmt.htm. (Retrieved on September 14, 2010)

Daulta, M. S. (2008), Impact of Home Environment on the Scholastic Achievement of Children, *Journal of Human Ecology*, 23 (1), 75-77.

Dave, P. N. (1974). The trend report. In M.B. Buch, Ed. (1974), *A survey of research in education*, Baroda: Case.

……….. & Anand, C. L. (1979). Correlates of achievement. In M.B. Buch, Ed. (1979), *Second Survey of research in education*, Baroda: SERD, 331.

David, K. D. & Stanley, H. L. (2000). Effect of Gender on Computer-based Chemistry Problem-solving. *Electronic Journal of Science Education, 4 (4).*

Davis, S. E., (2004). The role of students perceptions of classroom climate in predicting academic motivation and assigned grades in middle school mathematics. Published thesis. University of Florida.

Deary, I. J., Strand, S., Smith, P. & Fernandes, C., (2007) Intelligence and educational achievement, *Science Direct*, 35, (1), 13-21

Deci, E. L., Schwartz, A. Z., Sheinman, L. & Ryan, R.M. (1981). An instrument to assess adult's orientation toward control versus autonomy with children: Reflections on intrinsic motivation and perceived competence. *Journal of Educational Psychology.* 73. 642-650.

Den Brok P., Brekelmans, M., & Wubbels, T. (2004). Interpersonal teacher behavior and student outcomes, *School Effectiveness and School Improvement*, 15 (3 & 4): 407-422.

Deng, B. (1992). A multilevel analysis of classroom climate effects on mathematics achievement of fourth grade students (clearing house no. SEO 52843). Memphis, TN: Memphis State University. (ERIC Document Reproduction Service No. Ed. 348222).

Dettmer, J. (2005). Competition photography. . . learning by losing. *PSA Journal*, 36.

Dhanda P. B. & C. K. Singh (2009): Comparative Study of Intellectual Abilities of Rural and Urban Preschoolers, *Indian Psychological Review,* 72, (1) 45-48.

Diekhoe, M. & Wigginton P. K. (1992), Faculty perceptions of college classroom environment, *Studies in Higher Education,* 17 (1).

Dietrich, A., Bailey, E., (1996). School climate: Common sense solution to complicated problems, *Bulletin.* 16-17.

Din, Y. Y., Ming, M. C, & Esther S. H.˙ (2004). Hong Kong Students Achievement in OECD-PISA Study: Gender Differences in Science Content, Literary Skills, and Test Item Formats. *International Journal of Science and Mathematics Education, 2 (1),* 91106.

Dorman, J. P. (1997), Relationship between school level and classroom level environments in secondary schools, *Journal of educational administration*, 35 (1), 74-91.

.... (2008). Using student perception to compare actual and preferred classroom environment in Queensland schools, *Educational Studies* 34 (4), 299-308.

.... (2009). Some Determinants of Classroom Psychosocial Environment in Australian Catholic High Schools: A Multilevel Analysis, *A Journal of Inquiry and Practice*, 13(1).

.... Adams, J. E. and Ferguson, J. M. (2003). A cross national investigation of students perceptions of mathematics classroom environment and academic efficacy in secondary schools. *International Journal of Mathematics Teaching and Learning,* 15 April. [e-journal]

.... Fisher, D. L., Waldrip, B. G., (2002). Classroom environment, students, perceptions of assessment, academic efficacy and altitude to science: A LISREL analysis contemporary approaches to research on learning environments. World views world scientific publishing co. pvt. Ltd.

Eccles, J. S. (1993). School and family effects on the ontogeny of children's interests, self-perceptions, and activity choice. In J.Jacobs (Ed.), *Nebraska Symposium on Motivation: Vol. 40. Developmental perspectives on motivation* (pp.145–208): Lincoln: University of Nebraska Press

.... Lord, S. E., Roeser, R. W., Barber, B. L., & Jozefowwicz, D. M. (1997). The Association of School Transition in Early Adolescence with Developmental Trajectories through High School. In Schulenberg, J., Maggs, K., & Hurrelman, K. (Eds.*), Health Risks and Developmental Transitions during Adolescence (pp. 283-320).* New York: Cambridge University Press.

Ediger, M. (1996). Cooperative learning versus competition: Which is better? *Journal of Instructional Psychology,* 23, 204-300.

Edington, E. D. & Martellaro, H. C., (1984). Variables affecting academic achievement in New Mexico schools. Las Cruces: New Mexico Center for Rural Education. (Eric Document Reproduction Service No. 271 267).

Edmonds, R. & Fredriksen, J. (1979). Search for effective schools: The identification and analysis of schools that is instructionally effective for poor children (Clearing house no. UD019304). Detroit, MI:

Geographic Source (ERIC Document Reproduction Service No. ED 170396).

Ehrmann, N. & Massey, D. S. (2008) Gender-Specific Effects of Ecological Conditions on College Achievement, *Social Science Research*, 37 (1) 220-238.

Eleventh Five Year Plan, 2007-12, Volume-II, Social Sector, Planning Commission, Govt. of India, New Delhi, OUP, PP. 4 23 www.education.com Updated on Apr 18, 2011.

Elizabeth, J. F. (2009) *A Comparative Analysis of Family Structure and the Academic Achievement of African American Students in Selected Rural and Urban North Carolina High Schools* (Dissertation) *ETD Collection for Fayetteville State University*. Paper AAI3406577. http://digitalcommons.uncfsu.edu/dissertations/AAI3406577.

Emmons, C. L., Comer, J. P., & Haynes, N. M. (1996). Translating theory into practice: Comer's theory of school reform. In J. P. Comer, N. M. Haynes, E. Joyner, & M. Ben-Avie (Eds.), *Rallying the whole village* (pp. 27-41). New York: Teachers College Press.

Epstein, J. L., & Sheldon, S. B. (2002). Present and accounted for: Improving student attendance through family and community involvement. *Journal of Educational Research, 95,* 308-318.

Eshel, Y. & Kohavi, R. (2003). Perceived classroom control, self-regulated learning strategies and academic achievement, *Educational Psychology*, 23 (3), 249-260.

Eysenck, M. W. (2001). *Principles of cognitive psychology*. Hove, East Sussex: Psychology Press.

Eysenk, (2009). The effect of anxiety on academic achievement of students. Retrieved data on 15.07.2012 from http://www.sciencedaily.com/releases/2009/06/090623090713. Htm (In text citration Nadeem M. Ali A. Maqbool, S.; Zaidi, S.U. 2012).

Fagan, J. F., Holland, C. R., & Wheeler, K. (2007). The prediction, from infancy, of adult IQ and achievement. *Intelligence,* 35, (3), 225-231.

Fan, X. & Chen, M. J. (1999) Academic achievement of rural school students: A multi-year comparison with their peers in sub-urban and urban schools, *Journal of Research in Rural Education*, 15 (I) 31-46.

Farooq, M. S., Chaudhry, A. H., Shafiq, M. & Berhanu, G. (2011). Factors affecting students quality of academic performance: A case of secondary school level, *Journal of Quality and Technology Management,* VII (II), 01-14.

Fazal, S., Hussain, S., Mazoka, M. I., & Masood, S. (2012). The Role of Study Skill in Academic achievement of students: A closer focus on gender, *Pakistan Journal of Psychological Research, 27(1), 37-51.*

Felner, R. D., Aber, M. S., Primavera, J., & Cauce, A. M. (1985). Adaptation and vulnerability in high-risk adolescents: An examination of environmental mediators. *American Journal of Community Psychology*, 13, 365-379

Fergusson, D. M., & Horwood, L. J. (1997). Gender differences in educational achievement in a New Zealand birth cohort. *New Zealand Journal of Educational Studies*, 32(1) 83-96.

Fisher, D. L., & Khine, M. S. (Eds.). (2006). *Contemporary approaches to research on learning environments: Worldviews*. Singapore: World Scientific.

Fisher, D. L., Fraser, B. J., & Rickards, T. (1997). Gender and cultural differences in teacher-student interpersonal behavior, paper presented at the annual meeting of the American Educational Research Association, Chicago.

Fisher, D. L., Rickards, T, Goh, S.C., & Wong, A., (1997). 'Perceptions of interpersonal teacher behaviour in secondary science classrooms in Singapore and Australia', *Journal of Applied Research in Education,* 1, 3-11.

Fraine, B. D., Damme, J. V., & Onghena, P., (2007) "A Longitudinal Analysis of Gender Differences in Academic Self-Concept and Language Achievement: A Multivariate Multi Level Latent Growth Approach", *Contemporary Educational Psychology*, 32, (1) 132-150.

Fraser, B. J. (1981). Learning environment in curriculum evaluation: A review. Evaluation in education, *An International Review Series,* 5 (1), 3-93.

.... (1986). *Classroom environment.* London: Croom Helm.

.... (1989). *Assessing and improving classroom environment* (What Research Says, No. 2). Perth, Australia: Curtin University of Technology.

.... (1994). Research on classroom and school climate. In D. Gabel (Ed.), *Handbook of Research on Science Teaching and Learning,* (pp. 493-541). New York: Macmillan.

.... (1998 a). Classroom environment instruments: Development, validity, and applications, *Learning Environments Research, 1, 7-33.*

.... (1998 b). Science learning environment: assessment effects and determinants. *The International Handbook of Science Education*, 527-564.

.... (1998). Validity and use of classroom environment instruments. *Journal of Classroom Interaction,* 26, (2) 5-11.

.... (1984). The effect of classroom climate on student outcomes: A replication in to developing countries, Asia *Pacific Education*, 6 (2).

.... & Kawe, J. B. (2007). Classroom, home and peer environment influences on student outcomes in science and mathematics: an analysis of systematic reform data. *International Journal of Science Education,* 29, (15).

.... & Chionh, Y. H., (2000). *Classroom environment, self-esteem, achievement, and attitudes in geography and mathematics in Singapore.* Paper presented at the annual meeting of the American Educational Research Association, New Orleans, LA.

.... & Fisher, D. L. (1982). Predicting students outcomes from their perception of classroom psychological environments, *American Educational Research Journal*, 19, (4), 498-518.

.... Giddings, G. J., & McRobbie, C. J. (1995), 'Evolution and validation of personal forms of an instrument for assessing science laboratory classroom environments', *Journal of Research in Science Teaching,* 32, 339-422.

.... Walberg, H. C., Welch, W. W., & Hattice, J. A. (1987). Synthesis of educational productivity research. *International Journal of Educational Research,* 11, 145-252.

Freedman, M. P. (2002). The Influence of Laboratory Instruction on Science Achievement and Attitude towards Science across Gender Differences. *Journal of Women and Minorities in Science and Engineering, 8 (2),* 50.

Freiberg, H. J. (Ed) (1999). *School climate: Measuring, improving, and sustaining healthy learning environments.* London: Falmer Press.

Frieberg, J. (1998). Measuring school climate. *Educational Leadership*, 22-26.

Fuligni, A. J., Eccles, J. S., Barber, B. L. & Clements, P., (2001). Early adolescent peer engagement and adjustment during high school. *Developmental Psychology*, 37, 28-36.

Furong, S. & Limin, XIE (2008). On the urban-rural differences in classroom environment in compulsory education in the eastern coastal developed areas of China, *Frontier Education China,* 3 (2) 279-294.

Gagne, F. & Père, St. F. (2007). When IQ is controlled does Motivation Still Predict Achievement? *Intelligence,* 30, (1),

Gardiner, J. W. (1940). The relation of certain personality variables to level of aspiration. *Journal of Psychology*, 9, 191-206.

Garland, A. M. (2010). Assessing the relationship between student involvement and academic performance in higher education. Thesis, Western Kentucky University.

Gneezy, U., Niederle, M. & Rustichini, A., (2003). Performance in Competitive Environments: Gender Differences, *The Quarterly Journal of Economics*, 1051-1073.

Goh, S. C. & Khine, M. S. (2002). *Studies in educational learning environment: an international perspective*, Singapore, World Scientific Publisher.

Goh, S. C., & Fraser, B. J. (1996). Validation of an elementary school version of the questionnaire on teacher interaction. *Psychological Reports, 79,* 515-522.

Goodenow, C. (1993). Classroom belonging among early adolescent students: Relationships to motivation and achievement. *Journal of Early Adolescence*, 13, 21-43.

Goods, C. V. (1973). *Dictionary of Education*, Tata McGraw Hill Book Company, New York.

Graham, P. J. (1976). *The competitive emphasis of sport: A need for reflection.* Paper presented at the International Congress of Physical Activity Sciences, Quebec City, Quebec, CA.

Griffith, J. (1999). School climate as "social order" and "social action": A multi-level analysis of public elementary school student perceptions. *School Psychology of Education*, 2, 339 –369.

Guardino, C. A. & Fullerton, E. (2010). Changing behavirours by changing the classroom environment. *Teaching Exceptional Children*, 42 (6), 8-13.

Guilford, J. P. (1967) The nature of human intelligence. New York: MC Graw Hill.

Gupta, R. Sharma, S. & Gupta, M. (2012). A Study of Gender Difference on the Measure of Academic Achievement in Adolescent Students *VSRD-TNTJ, 3 (1)* 23-27,

Gurubasappa, H. D. (2009). Intelligence and self-concept as correlates of academic achievement of secondary school students, *Edutracks*. 8, (10) 42-43.

Habibollah, N., Rohani, A., Tengku Aizan, H. & Jamaluddin, S. V., (2010) Intelligence and academic achievement: an investigation of gender differences, *Life Science Journal*, 7, (1).

.... & Mallan, K. (2009) Gender Differences in Creative, Perceptions of Undergraduate Students, *Journal of Applied Sciences,* 9, (1), 167-172.

Hallinan, M. T. (2008). Teacher influences on students' attachment to school. *Sociology of Education,* 81(3), 271-283.

Halpin A. W. & Craft, D. B. (1963) *The organizational climate of school.* Chicago: Midwest. Administration Centre of the University Chicago.

Hamilton, D., Hinton, L., & Qian, D. (2008). International students: Does attendance an indicator of involvement correlate with assessment performance? In proceedings of *Lifelong Learning Conference* (Publisher) (pp. 188-194). Retrieved July 20, 2010,fromhttp://researchbank. swinburne.edu.au/vital/ access/manager/Repository/swn.

Hancock, D. R. (2001). Effect of test anxiety and evaluative threats on students achievement and motivation. *The Journal of Educational Research* 94 (5), 284-290.

Hanrahan, M. (1998). The effect of learning environment factors on students motivation and learning, *International Journal of Science Education* 20 (6) 733-753.

Hanson, S. L. (1994). Lost talent: Unrealized educational aspirations and expectations among U.S. youths. *Sociology of Education,* 67, 159-183.

Harris, J. A. (2004). Measured intelligence, achievement, openness to experience, and creativity. *Personality and Individual Differences, 36*, 913-929.

Hartel, G. D., Walberg, H., G., & Hartel, E. H. (1981). Socio-psychological environments and learning: A quantitative synthesis. *British Educational Research Journal,* 7, 27-36.

Harter, S. (1999). *The Construction of Self: A Developmental Perspective.* New York: Guilford.

Haveman, R., & Wolfe, B. (1995). The determinants of children's attainments: A review of methods and findings. *Journal of Economic Literature, 33,* 1829–1878.

Hearn, J. C., Moos R. H., (1978). Subject matter and classroom climate: A test of Holland's environmental propositions. *American Educational Research Journal.* 1978; 15:111–124.

Henderson, D., Fisher, D. L. & Fraser, B. J. (2000). 'Interpersonal behaviour, laboratory learning environments, and student outcomes in senior biology classes, *Journal of Research in Science Teaching,* vol. 37, pp. 26-43.

Hillman, K., & Rothman, S. (2003). *Gender differences in educational and labour market outcomes.* Melbourne: Australian Council for Educational Research.

Hoff, E., Laursen, B., & Tardif, T. (2002). Socioeconomic status and parenting. In M. H. Bornstein (Ed.), *Handbook of Parenting* (2) 231–252. Mahwah, NJ: Lawrence Erlbaum Associates, Inc.

Hong, E. & Lee, K. H. (2000). Preferred homework style and homework environment in high-versus low achieving Chinese students. *Educational Psychology.* 26, 125-137.

Hopson, M., Richard L., Simms & Gerald A Knezek (2002). Using a technology enriched environment to improve higher order thinking skills, *Journal of Research on Technology in Education,* 34, (2).

Horn, L. J. & Carroll C. D. (1997). Confronting the odds: students at risk and the pipeline to higher education (Statistical Analysis Report). (National Center for Education Statistics No. NCES 98-094.

House of Representatives Standing Committee on Education and Training (2002). *Boys: Getting it right. Canberra: Commonwealth Government.* Office for Standards in Education (2003). Boys' achievement in secondary schools. London: OFSTED Publications Centre.

House, J. (2000). The effects of student involvement on the development of an academic self-concept. *Journal of Social Psychology,* 140, 261-263.

Howley, C. (2002) "Research about Mathematics Achievement in Rural Circumstance", Working Paper, No. 4, Appalachian Collaborative

Centre for the Study of Learning, Assessment and Instruction in Mathematics, Athens, Ohio University, Ohio, 2002.

Hunus, R., & Fraser, B. J. (1997). Chemistry learning environment in Brunei Darussalam's secondary schools. In D.L. Fisher, and T. Rickards (Eds.), science, mathematics and technology education and national development. Proceedings of the Vietnam Conference (PP. 108-120). Hanoi; Vietnam.

Hurlock, E. B. (1967), *Adolescent Development*, New York: McGrow HillCo.Inc.

Hutty, K. (2004). Alexander Austin's Theory of Involvement: A summary. http://www.cat.ilstu.edu/conf/astin.shtml.

Hyde, J. S., & Linn, M. C. (2006). Gender similarities in mathematics and science. *Science,* 314, (5799), 599-600.

Hyde, J. S., Fennema, E., & Lamon, S. J. (1990). Gender differences in mathematics performance: A meta-analysis. *Psychological Bulletin*, 107(2), 139-155.

Hyde, J. S., McKinley, N. M. (1997). Gender Difference in Cognition. Results from Meat-analysis. In Caplan, P.J., Crawford, M., Hyde, J.S. & Richardson, J.T.E. (Eds.), *Gender Differences in Human Cognition (pp 30-51).* New York: Oxford Press.

Jacobs, N. & Harvey, D. (2005). Do parents make a difference to children's academic achievement? Differences between parents of higher and lower achieving students, *Educational Studies*, 31(4), 431–448.

Jacobson L. T. & Burdsal C. A. (2012). Academic performance in middle school: Friendship Influences. *Global Journal of Community psychology practice.* 2(3) 1-12.

Jayshree, C. (2006) Influence of classroom climate on academic achievement of learners in secondary schools Dissertation, University of Zululand.

Jencks, C., Crouse, J. & Mueser, P. (1983). The Wisconsin Model of Status Attainment: A national replication with improved measures of ability and aspiration. *Sociology of Education,* 56 (1), 3-19.

Jimerson, S., Egeland, B., & Teo, A. (1999). A longitudinal revise of achievement trajectories factors associated with change. *Journal of Educational Psychology, 91,* 116–126.

Jindal S. K. (1976) Student perception of college environment as Related to their satisfaction in college of Haryana, Kurukshetra University Ph.D. Thesis.

Joshi, M. C., & Vyas, O. P. (1997). *Technical booklet and manual of directions for classroom environment scale*, Rupa Psychological Center, Varanasi.

Joshi, S & Srivastava, R., (2009): Self-esteem and academic achievement of adolescents *Journal of the Indian Academy of Applied Psychology*, 35, 33-39.

Juvonen, J., & Wentzel, K. R. (1996). *Social motivation: Under-standing children's school adjustment.* New York: Cambridge University Press.

Karim, N. S. & Hassan, A. (2006). Reading Habits and Attitude in the Digital age: Analysis of gender and academic program differences in Malaysia. *The Electronic Library*, Vol. 25, No. 3, p. 288-297.

Kentucky Council on Post-Secondary Education (2007). One year system Wide Retention of First time Freshmen. Retrieved August 11, 2008 from http://cpe.ky.gov/info/ retention.

Ketika, T. & Indrani, V. (2013). Influence of Constructivism in Teaching on Academic Achievement of Primary Students, *Journal of Education & Research for Sustainable Development*, Volume-1 (1), 1.

Khalid, R. & Hasan, S. S. (2009). Text anxiety in high and low achievers. *Pakistan Journal of Psychological Research,* 24 (3-4).

Khan, S., Anila, & Pervez, S. (1991). Adaptation of Home Inventory (Infant version) for Pakistani Children. *Pakistan Journal of Psychological Research*, 6, 13-23.

Khetrapal, I. (2002), Classroom management, *Encyclopedia of Indian education*, Vol I (A-K).

Kiany, G. R., & Shayestefar, P. (2011). High school students perceptions of EFL teacher control orientations and their English academic achievement. *British Journal of Educational Research.* 81(3), 491-508.

Kim, H. B. & Fisher, D. L., & Frasher, B. J. (2000). Classroom environment and teacher interpersonal behaviour in secondary science classes in Korea. *Evaluation & Research in Education,* 14, (1),

Kim, H., Fisher, D. L., & Fraser, B. J. (1999). Assessment and investigation of constructivist science learning environments. *Research in Science and Technological Education, 17,* 239–249.

King, M. (2006). Finding balance. *Campus Activities Programming*, 38(6).

Klebanov, P. K., Brooks-Gunn, J., & Duncan, G. J. (1994). Does neighborhood and family poverty affect mothers' parenting, mental health, and social support? *Journal of Marriage and the Family, 56,* 441–455.

Knight, S. L., Waxman, H. C., & Padron, Y.N. (1989). Examining the relationship between classroom instruction and elementary students' cognitive strategies in social studies. *Journal of Educational Research*, 82(5), 270-276.

Knight, S. L., Waxman, H. C., & Sterchy, S., Y. N. (1990). Effects of the classroom learning environment on high school students motivation. *Southwest Journal of Educational Research,* (3), 28-34.

Kobal, D. & Musek, J. (2001). Self-concept and academic achievement: Slovenia and France. *Personality and Individual Differences,* volume 30(5)887-899.

Koke, L. C. & Vernon P. A. (2003) "The Sternberg Triarchic Abilities Test (STAT) as a Measure of Academic Achievement and General Intelligence", *Personality and Individual Differences,* 35, (8), 1803-1807.

Kolawole, E.B. (2007). Effects of Competitive and Cooperative Learning Strategies on Academic Performance of Nigerian Students in Mathematics. *Educational Research Review, 3 (1)*, 33-37.

Kossowska, S. (1999). Learning Styles, Differential Effects of Self-Control and Deep-Level Information Processing on Academic Achievement, *Personality Psychology in Europe*, 7, 263-281.

Koul R. B. &, Fisher D. L. (2002). Science classroom learning environments in India. Paper presented at the International Educational Research Conference of the Australian Association for Research in Education (AARE), Brisbane, Australia.

Kuperminc, G. P., Leadbeater, B. J., & Blatt, S. J. (2001). School social climate and individual differences in vulnerability to psychopathology among middle school students. *Journal of School Psychology*, 39, 141-159.

Kuperminc, G. P., Leadbeater, B. J., Emmons, C., & Blatt, S. J. (1997).Perceived school climate and difficulties in the social adjustment of middle school students. *Applied Developmental Science,* 1, 76-88.

Kusurkar, R. A., Ten Cate, Th. J., Vos, C. M. P., Westers, P. & Croiset, G. (2013). How motivation affects academic performance a structural equalism modeling analysis. *Advances in Health Sciences Education*, 18(1): 57-69 Mar 2013. Available at: http://www.cric.com.

Laidra, K., Pullman, H. & Allik, J. (2007). Personality and intelligence as predictor of academic achievement: A cross sectional study from elementary to secondary school. *Personality and Individual Differences*, 42(3), 67-83.

Lam, S, Yim, P., Law, J., & Cheung, R. (2004). The effects of competition on achievement motivation in Chinese classrooms. *British Journal of Educational Psychology*, 74(2). 281-296.

Lama, M. Al-Qaisy (2011) The relation of depression and anxiety in academic achievement among group of university students *International Journal of Psychology and Counseling* 3(5), 96-100.

Lau, K. L. & Lee, J. C. K. (2008). Examining Hong Kong students achievement goals and their relations with students perceived classroom environment and strategy use. *Educational Psychology, 28, 357-372.*

Lavin, D. E. (1965). *The prediction of academic performance.* New York Russell. Sage Foundation

Lawrenz, F. P. (1987). Gender effects for student perceptions of the classroom psychosocial environment. *Journal of Research in Science Teaching, 24* (8), 689-697.

Lee, V., Bryk, A., & Smith, J. (1993). The Organization of Effective Secondary Schools. *Review of Research in Education*, 19, 171-267

Lim, T. K. (1995) Perception of classroom environment, school types, gender and learning styles of secondary school students, *Educational Psychology* 15, (2), 1995.

Lubbers, M. J. (2006). The impact of peer relation on academic progress in junior high. *Journal of School Psychology.* 44, 49-512.

Luster, T., Rhoades, K., & Haas, B. (1989). The relation between parental values and parenting behavior: A test of the Kohn Hypothesis. *Journal of Marriage and the Family, 51,* 139–147.

Ma, X. (2003). Sense of belonging to school: Can school make a difference? *The Journal of Educational Research,* 96(6), 340-349.

Mac Aulay, D. J. (1990). Classroom environment: A literature review. *Educational Psychology*, 10 (3), 239-253.

Mac Intosh, J. (1991). Dimensions and determinants of school climate in schools enrolling middle year's students. (online) available: http//www.ssta.sk.ca /research/school improvement/91-04. Htm#K.

Maehr, M. L. & Midgley, C. (1991). Restructuring the school environment to enhance student motivation and learning. *American Educational Research Association Annual Meeting*, 2-18.

Mahony, P. & Hextall, I. (2000). *Reconstructing teaching: Standards, performance and accountability.* New York: Routledge Falmer.

Margianti, E. S., Fraser, B. J., & Aldridge, J. M. (2001, December). Investigating the Learning Environment and Students Outcomes at the University Level in Indonesia. Paper Presented at the Annual Meeting of the Australian Association for Research in Education (AARE), Fremantle, Western Australia.

Marsh, H. W. (1989). Age and sex effects in multiple dimensions of self-concept: Preadolescence to early adulthood. *Journal of Educational Psychology*, 81, 417-430.

.... (1990a). Causal ordering of academic self-concept and academic achievement: A Multiwave, longitudinal panel analysis. *Journal of Educational Psychology. 82*(4), 646-656.

.... & Craven, R. (1997). Academic self-concept: Beyond the dustbowl. In G. Phye (Ed.), *Handbook of Classroom Assessment: Learning, Achievement, and Adjustment.* Orlando, FL: Academic.

.... & Hau, K. (2003). Big-fish-little-pond-effect on academic self-concept. A cross cultural (26country) test of the negative effects of academically selective schools. *American Psychologist, 58*(5), 364-376.

Marzano, R. J., & Marzano, J. s. (2003).The key to classroom management, *Educational Leadership*, 61(1), 6-13.

Masson, A. M., Hoyois, P., Pcadot, M., Nahama, V., Petit, F., & Ansseau, M. (2004). Girls are more successful than boys at the university: Gender group differences in models integrating motivational and aggressive components correlated with test-anxiety. [Online] Available: http://www.ncbi.nlm.nih.gov/sites/entrez?db=journals&term.

Masutha, M. R. & Ackermann, C. J. (1999). Secondary School students perception of their teachers. *South African Journal of Education,* 19 (3), 243-248.

Mayes, S. D., & Calhoun, S. L. (2007a). Learning, attention, writing, and processing speed in typical children and children with ADHD, autism, anxiety, depression, and oppositional-defiant disorder. Child Neuropsychology: *A Journal on Normal and Abnormal Development in Childhood and Adolescence,* 13(6), 469-493.

Mayes, S. D., & Calhoun, S. L. (2007b). Wechsler Intelligence Scale for Children-Third and-Fourth Edition predictors of academic achievement in children with attention-deficit/hyperactivity disorder. *School Psychology Quarterly*, 22(2), 234-249.

Mc Rubbie, C. J. Roth, W.M. & Lucus, K.B. (1997). Multiple learning environments in a physics classroom. *International Journal of Educational Research,* 27.

McGrew, K. S., & Flanagan, D. P. (1997). Beyond g: The impact of Gf-Gc specific cognitive abilities research on the future use and *School. Psychology Review, 26* (2), 189.

Miller, S. I., & Fredericks, J. (1990). The false ontology of school climate effects. *Educational Theory*, 40, 333–342.

Monroe Community College (2004). Campus Center Mission. Retrieved June 14, 2004, from http: www.monroecc.edu/dept/stucenter/mission htm.

Montalvo, G. P., Mansfield, E. A., & Miller, R. B. (2007). Liking or disliking the teacher: Student motivation, engagement and achievement. *Evaluation and Research in Education,* 20(3), 144-158.

Moos, R. & Trickett, E. J. (1974). *Classroom environment scale.* Consulting psychological press, Palo Alto, California.

Moos, R. (1979). *Evaluating educational environments: Procedures, measures, findings, and policy implications.* San Francisco: Jossey-Bass.

Moos, R., & Moos, B. (1978). Classroom social climate and student absences and grades. *Journal of Educational Psychology*, 70, 263-269.

Mudasir, H. & Yatu, D. S. (2012). A comparative study of intelligence and academic achievement of Kashmiri and Tibetan students. *Scholarly Journal of Education* Vol. 1(5), 76-80.

Mullis, I. V. S., Martin, M. O., Gonzalez, E. J., & Kennedy, A. M. (2003). PIRLS 2001 international report: IEA's study of reading literacy achievement in primary schools. Chestnut Hill, MA: Boston College.

Myint, S. K. & Goh, S. C. (2001). Investigation of tertiary classroom learning environment. In Singapore, Paper Presented at the International Educational Research Conference. Australian Association for Educational Research (AARE), University of Notre Dame, Fremantle Western Australia.

Nadeem, M.; Ali, A.; Maqbool, S. & Zaidi, S. U. (2012). Impact of anxiety on the academic achievement of students having different mental abilities at university level in Bahawalpur (Southern Punjab), Pakistan, *International Online Journal of Educational Sciences.* 4 (3), 519-528.

Naderi, H., Abdullah, R., Aizan, H. T. & Sharir, J. (2010). Intelligence and academic achievement: An Investigation of Gender Differences, *Life Science Journal* 7(1), 83-87.

Nagaraju, M. T. V. Sumalatha, K Reddy, V.G. (2003): Academic Achievement in Relation to Certain Factors, *The Educational Review*, 46, (2), 46-50.

Naglieri J. A., & Bornstein B. T., (2003) Intelligence and Achievement: Just how Correlated are they? *Journal of Psycho Educational Assessment*, 21, (3), 244-260.

Nandita & Tanima, S. (2004). Study habits and attitude towards studies in relation to academic achievement. *Psycho-Lingua*, 34 (1)57-60.

Nanson-Salton stall, M. (2004). Involvement equals retention. Retrieved June, 2004 from NAVSS student Affairs Datamart.

National Assessment of Educational Progress (NAEP) (2011) From Wikipedia, the free encyclopedia, http://en.wikipedia.org /wiki/ National_Assessment_of_ Educational_Progress

Needham, B. L. (2006). Gender differences in the consequences of depressive symptomatology for educational attainment, social support, and health risk behavior during the transition from adolescence to young adulthood, Unpublished PhD thesis, University of Texas.

Neisser, U., *et. al.* (1996). Intelligence: Known and Unknowns. *American Psychologist, 51*(2), 77-101.

Newman, R. S., & Schwager, M. T. (1993). Student perceptions of the teacher and classmates in relation to reported help seeking in math class. *Elementary School Journal*, 94, 3-17.

Nicholson, A. M. (2009). Effects of test anxiety on student achievement (ACT) for college bound students. Dissertation Abstract International, DAI-A-70/07, AAT 3366126.

Nielson, H.; Kirk, D. (1974). Classroom climate. In H.J. Walberg (Ed.), *Evaluating Educational Performance: A Sourcebook of Methods, Instruments, and Examples.* Berkeley, CA: Mc Cutchan.

Nneji L. (2002). *Study Habits of Nigerian University Students.* HERDSA conference.http://www.ecu.edu.au/conferences/herdsa/main /papers / ref/pdf/Nneji

No Child Left Behind Act of 2001. Pub. L. No. 107-110,

Nouhi, E., Shakoori, A. & Nakhei, N. (2008). Study habits and skills and academic achievement of students in Kerman University of Medical Sciences, *Journal of Medicine Education,* 12 (3, 4), 77-80.

Nuthana, P. G. & Yenagi, G. V. (2009): Influence of study habits, self-concept on achievement of boys and girls. *Karnataka Journal of Agricultural Sciences,* 22(5), 1135-1138

Obe, Eo., (1984) Urban rural and sex difference in scholastic aptitude on primary school finalist Lagos state. *Education and development*, 41(2), 123-134.

Office for Standards in Education (2003) *Leadership and Management: What Inspection Tells us.* Document No. HMI 1646. London: OFSTED.

Oganshola, F. & Adewale, A. M. (2012). The effect of parental socio-economic status on academic performance of students in selected schools in Edu Lga of Kwara state Nigeria. *International Journal of Academic Research in Bussiness and Social Sciences*, 2 (7), 230-239.

Okoh, A. S. (2011). Comparison between perceptions of classroom environment by biology students in public and private secondary schools PGDE project, University of Port Harcourt, Nigeria.

Okonkwo, C. (2010). Relationship between secondary school students perceptions of classroom learning environment and their achievement in chemistry. PGDE Project, University of Port Harcourt, Nigeria.

Okpala, C. O., A. O., & Smith, F. E. (2001). Parental involvement, instructional expenditures, family socio-economics attributes, and student achievement. *Journal of Educational Research,* 95(2), 110-115.

Okurat, O. C. (2010): Classroom learning environment and motivation towards mathematics among secondary school students in Uganda. *Learning environment Research*, 13: 267-277.

Olatoye, R. A. (2004a). Interest in schooling as a determinant of Secondary School Students Study Habit. *International Journal of Literacy Education.* Published by Adult Education Department, University of Ibadan.

.... & Ogunkola, B. J. (2009). Parental involvement, interest in schooling and science achievement of junior secondary school students in Ogun State, Nigeria. *Educational Research and Review*, 4(10), 457-464.

Oludipe, (2009). Influence of text anxiety on performance levels on numerical tasks of secondary school physics students, *Academic Leadership*, *Online Journal*, 7 (4).

……….. Daniel I. (2012) Gender Difference in Nigerian Junior Secondary Students Academic Achievement in Basic Science, *Journal of Educational and Social Research,* 2 (1), 93-99.

Oluwatimileim, J. T. B. & Owoyele, J. W. (2012). Study habits and academic achievement in core subjects among junior secondary school students in Ondo State, Nigeria, *Bulgarian Journal of Science and Education Policy* (BJSEP) 6 (1), 155-169.

Onwuegbuzie, A. J., Slate, J. R., & Schwartz, R. A. (2001). The role of study skills in graduate-level educational research courses. *Journal of Educational Research*, 94, 238-246.

Osterman, K. (2000). Students need for belonging in the school community. *Review of Educational Research*, 70 (3), 323-367.

Owens, L. E. & Straton, R. G. (1980) The development of a cooperative, competitive and individualised learning preference scale for students', *British Journal of Educational Psychology,* 50,147-161.

Owoeye, J. S. (2002). The effect of integration of location, facilities and class size on academic achievement of secondary school students in Ekiti State University, Nigeria. Unpublished Ph.D Dissertation, University of Ibadan, Nigeria.

Ozturk, M. A. & Debelak, C. (2005) Setting Realistically High Academic Standards, http://www.usca.edu/essays/vol152005/ozturkrev.pdf Accessed on 17thDecember 2011.

Padma, M. S . (1991). Research in correlates of achievement, In M.B. Buch, Ed. (1991), Fourth survey of research in education, New Delhi: NCERT, 807.

Pamela, E. Davis-Kean (2005) The influence of parent education and family income on child achievement: The indirect role of parental expectations and the home environment, *Journal of Family Psychology*, 19, (2), 294–304.

Panigrahi, M. N. (2005) Academic achievement in relation to intelligence and socio-economic status. *Edutrack*, 5(2), 26-27.

Parveen, A. & Alam, M. T. (2008) Does Mothers' Education Influence Children's Personality Factors and Academic Achievement? *Bulletin of Education and Research,* 30, (2) 1-6.

Parveen, A. Syed, N. A. & Syed, K. N. (2013). Comparative study of the academic achievement of 10th class boys and girls studying in different high schools of district Pulwama (J & K) of *Journal of Educational Research and behavioral science*. Vol. 2 (2) 020-027.

Pascarella, E. & Terenzini, P. (1991). *How College Affects Students*, San Francisco, CA: Jossey Bass.

Pianta, R., Belsky, J., Vandergrift, N., Houts, R., & Morrison, F. (2008).Classroom effects on children's achievement trajectories in elementary school. *American Educational Research Journal,* 45, 365–397.

Praat, A. (1999). Gender differences in student achievement and in rates of participation in the school sector, 1986-1997: a summary report. *The Research Bulletin,* 10, 1-11.

Pretorius, F. (1998). *Outcomes-Based Education in South Africa*: Hodderand Stoughton.

Ramaswamy, R. (1990). Study habits and academic achievement. Expt. Edu., Relation to their sex intelligence and socio-economic. 18(10) 255-260 status. *Fourth Survey Education Research.* P. 895.

Rana, R. A., Mahmood, N., (2010). The relationship between text anxiety and academic achievement, *Bulletin of Education and Research,* 32(2), 63-74.

Rao, N. Moely, B. E. & Sachs, J. (2000). Motivational beliefs, study strategies, and mathematic attainment in high and low achieving Chinese secondary school students. *Contemporary educational psychology,* 25, 287-316.

Renninger, K. A., Hidi, S., Krapp, A. (Eds) (1992). *The role of interest in learning and development. Hilsdale,* N: Erlbaum, 361-395.

Rhea, A., & Otto, L. (2001). Mothers' influence on adolescents' educational outcome beliefs. *Journal of Adolescent Research,* 16(5), 491-510. Right to Education Act. (2009).

Rohd, T. E. & Thompson, L. A. (2007). Predicting academic achievement with cognitive ability. *Intelligence,* 35(1), 83-92.

Rohen Meetei. (2012). A critical study of impact of academic anxiety on academic achievement of class ixth students. http://www.scribd.com/doc/23767970/A-Ciritical-Study-of-Impact-of-Academic-Anxiety-onAcademic-Achievement-of-Class-Ixth-Students-Bareilly.

Roscigno, Vincent J. & Martha Crowley. 2001. Rurality, Institutional Disadvantage, and Achievement/Attainment. *Rural Sociology,* 66 (2), 268-293.

Royce, S. B. (2009). Grade integrity and the representation of academic achievement. *Studies in Higher Education,* 34 (7) 807-826.

Rumberger, R.W. (1983). Dropping out of high school: The influence of race, sex and family background. *American Educational Research Journal,* 20(2), (199-220).

Ryan, A. M., & Patrick, H. (2001). The classroom social environment and changes in adolescents' motivation and engagement during middle school. *American Educational rsearch Journal,* 38, 437-460.

Ryan, R. M. & Powelson, C. L. (1991). Autonomy and relatedness as fundamental to motivation in education. *Journal of experimental education.* 60. 49-66.

Ryan, H., & Patric, A. M., (2006). Identifying adaptive classrooms: analyses of measures of dimensions of the classroom social environment, Paper prepared for the Positive Outcomes Conference, March 2003 Post-conference Revised Version, May 2003.

Sadeghi A. (2010). Affecting the classroom psychological environment (CPE) on approaches of student learning in guilan university, Iran procedia- *social and behaviour science,* 5, 1301-1306.

Saini, M. (2013). A study of academic achievement of scheduled caste secondary school students in relation to study habits, home environment and school environment Ph.D. thesis, Maharishi Dayaand University, Department of Education.

Saleh, I. AL., *et. al.,* (2001). "Relationships between Blood Lead Concentrations, Intelligence, and Academic Achievement of Saudi Arabian School Girls*", International Journal of Hygiene and Environmental Health,* 204(2-3), 165-174.

Samuel, W.W. & John, G.M. (2004). Effects of Cooperative Class Experiment Teaching Method on Secondary School Students Chemistry Achievement in Kenya's Nakuru District. *International Education Journal, 5 (1)*, 26-35.

Sandra, D., (2004). Classroom goal orientation in high school classrooms: revealing links between teacher beliefs and classroom environments, *Educational Research, 46(1)73.*

Savage, T. V. (1999). *Teaching self-control through management and discipline.* Boston: Allyn and Bacon.

Schibeci R. A. & Fraser B. J. (1987). Effect of classroom environment on science student: A cross-cultural replication in Indonesia. *International Journal of Science Education,* 9, (2), 1987

Schiefele, U., & Csikszentmihalyi, M., (1995). Motivation and ability as factors in mathematics experience and achievement. *Journal for Research in Mathematics Education,* 26(2), 163-181.

Sharma, S. (1982), "A Study of the Leadership Behaviour of Headmasters vis a vias the School climate" PhD Thesis, Edu. Agra Uni.

Sharmistha (2008). A comparative study of factors affecting academic achievement of school going adolescent boys and girls. Paper presentation, Department of Human Development and Family Studies, Faculty of Family Community Science, Maharaja Sayajirao University of Baroda, Gujarat, India.

Shavelson, R. J., Hubner, J. J. & Stanton, G. C. (1976). Self-concept: Validation of construct interpretations. *Review of Educational Research*, 46(3), 407-441.

Shochet, I. M., Dadds, M. R., Ham, D., & Montague, R. (2006). School connectedness is an underemphasized parameter in adolescent mental health: Results of a community prediction study. Journal of *Clinical Child and Adolescent Psychology*, 35, 170 –179

Sing, S. (2012). A study of academic achievement of IXth class students of district Solan of Himachal Pradesh in relation to their area of residence and self-concept Shodh. Samiksha Aor Mulagankan. *International Indeyed referred Journal* April, 2012. Vol. IV, Issue 39.

Singh, A. & Singh, A. K., (2007) Impact of caste sex and habitat on achievement in Mathematics at upper primary school. *Journal of Teacher Education and Research*, 2(2).23-27.

Singh, R.D.(1983) A Study of deprivation, achievement and level of aspiration in High School Students of Science Group, Ph.D. Ph. D. Thesis, Harising Gor. University.

Sirin, S. R., (2005). Socioeconomic status and academic achievement: A meta-analytic review of research. *Review of Educational Research*, 75(3), 417-453.

Smith, J. R., Brooks-Gunn, J., & Klebanov, P. K., (1997) Consequences of living in poverty for young children's cognitive and verbal ability and early school achievement. In G. J. Duncan & J. Brooks-Gunn (Eds.), *Consequences of growing up poor* (pp.132–189). New York: Russell Sage Foundation.

Spearman, C. (1927). *The Abilities of Man.* London: MacMillan.

Spelke, E. S. (2005). Sex differences in intrinsic aptitude for mathematics and science? A critical review. *American Psychologist*, 60(9), 950-958.

Stanly V. J. (2005) Role of thinking style in educational performance: A study among tribal non-tribal students of Bastar district. Ph. d. Thesis, Pt. Ravishankar Shukla University.

Steinberge, L. *et. al.,* (1984). Dropping out among language minority youth. *Review of Educational Research,* 54(1), (113-132).

.... Dornbusch, S. M. & Brown, B. B. (1992). Ethenic differences in adolescent achievement: An ecological perspective. *American psychologist*, 47, 723-729.

.... Lamborn, S. D., Dornbusch, S. M. & Darling, N. (1992) Impact of parenting practices on adolescent achievement: authoritative parenting, school involvement and encouragement to succeed, *Child Development,* 63, 1266–1281.

Steinberger, E. D. (1993) *Improving Student* Achievement, Virginia: American of School Administrators.

Steinmayr, R., Zieglar, M. & Trauble, B. (2010) "Do intelligence and sustained attention interact in predicting academic achievement?" *Learning and Individual Difference*, 20, (1), retrieved from, http//www.sciencedirect.com, accessed on 12 May 2010.

Stern, G. C. (1970). People in context: Measuring person–environment congruence in education and industry. New York: John Wiley.

Sternberg, *et. al.,* (2001).The relationship between academic and practical intelligence: a case study in Kenya. *Intelligence, 29* (5), 401-41.

Stewart, S. C. & Evans, W. H. (1997). Setting the stage for success: Assessing the instructional environment. *Preventing School Failure*, 41(2), 53-56.

Steyn, G.M. (2001). Focusing on guiding principles of quality to redesign educational institutions. *South African, Journal of Education.* 21

Sudhir, M. A & Lalhirimi, S. (1989). Parent Child interaction and achievement among Secondary School students in Aizwi. *Psychological Abstract* 78(1).

Suleman, Q., Aslam, H.D., Hussain, I., Shakir, M. & Nisa Zaib-un (2012). Effects of parental socio-economic status on the academic achievement of secondary school students in district Karak (Pakistan). *International Journal of Human Resource Studies*, 2 (4).

Sungur, S. & Gungoren, S. (2009) The role of classroom environment perceptions in self-regulated learning and science achievement. *Elementary education online,* 8 (3) 883-900.

Sungur, S. & Tekkaya, C. (2003). Students Achievement in Human Circulatory System Unit: the Effect of Reasoning Ability and Gender. *Journal of Science Education and Teaching, 12 (1)*, 59-64.

Suzanna Mokhtar (2003) Classroom environment and academic performance at kolej yayasan pelajaran mara kuala lumpur, Ph. d, Thesis, International Islamic University Malaysia.

Taj, H. (1999). Academic achievement as a function of social-class, parent-child interaction, dependency behavior and school management. *Psycho Lingua,* 29(2), 153-158.

Talton E.L. & Simpson R. D. (1987), Relationships of attitude towards classroom environment with altitude toward and achievement in science among tenth grade biology students *Journal of reserve in science teaching,* 24, (6), 507-525.

Teachman, J. D. (1987) Family background, educational resources and educational attainment, *American Sociological Review*, 52, 548–557.

Tella, A. (2007) The impact of motivation of student's academic achievement and learning outcomes in Mathematics among secondary school students in Nigeria Eurasia *Journal of Mathematics, Science and Technology Education*, 3 (2), 149-156.

Tella, A., Tella, A., & Adeniy, O. (2009) Locus of control, interest in schooling, self-efficacy and academic Achievement, *Cypriot Journal of Educational Sciences,* 4 (3) 168-182.

Thiessen, V., & Nickerson, C. (1999). Canadian gender trends in education and work, Ottawa: Human Resources Development Canada Applied Research Branch.

Thompson, M., Alexander, K., & Entwisle, D. (1988). Household composition, parental expectations, and school achievement. *Social Forces*, 67, 424-451.

Thursetone, L. L. (1932) *Primary Mental Abilities*. Chicago, University of Chicago Press.

Trickett, E. J., & Moos, R. H. (1973). Social environment of junior high and high school classrooms. *Journal of Educational Psychology*, 65, 93-102.

Tucker, C. M., Harris, Y. R., Brady, B. A., & Herman, K. C. (1996). The association of selected parent behaviors with the academic achievement of African American children and Caucasian children. *Child Study Journal*, 26(4), 253-277.

Tucker, C. M., Zayco, R. A., & Herman, K. C. (2002). Teacher and child variables as predictors of academic engagement among low-income African American children. *Psychology in the Schools, 39*(4), 477-488.

U. S. Department of Education (2002), National Center for Education Statistics, The Condition of Education 2002, NCES 2002–025, Washington, DC: U.S. Government Printing Office.

Uniyal, M. P. (2007) Co-relation Study of Level of Aspiration and Scholastic Achievement in Relation to Sex and Caste. *Journal of Teacher Education and Research,* NewDelhi. 2, (2), 67-74.

Useem, E. L. (1992) Middle schools and maths groups: parents involvement in children's placement, *Sociology of Education,* 65, 263–279.

Usha, P. (2007): Emotional adjustment and family acceptance of the child, correlates for achievement, *Edutracks,* .6, (No) 10, 25-27.

Ushakumari M. B. (2008). Relationship of teacher aptitude with academic achievement and certain psychological variables of primary Teacher trainees of Kerala. Ph.D. Thesis, University of Calicut.

Vaidya, S. A. (2006). A study of educational aspiration of higher secondary students in relation to different variables. Ph.D. (Edu.), Gujarat University.

VanLaar, C., & Sidarius, J. (2001). Social status and the academic achievement gap: A social dominance perspective. *Social Psychology of Education,* 4(3-4), 235-258.

Vernon, P. A 1971) *The Structure of Human Abilities*. LONDON: Methuen.

Walberg, H. (1971). Model of optimizing and individualizing school learning, *Interchang*, 3, 15-27.

Walberg, H. (1979). *Educational environments and effects; evaluation, policy, and productivity*. Berkeley, CA: Mc Cutchan.

Walker, H. M. & Walker, J. E. (1991). Coping with noncompliance in the classroom: A positive approach for teachers. Austin, TX: Pro-Ed.

Walker, H. M., Colvin, G., & Ramsey, E. (1995). *Anti-social behavior in school: Strategies and best practices.* Pacific Grove, CA: Brooks/Cole Publishing Company.

Wang Shiung Kwei & Thomas C. (2006) The effects of a web based learning environment on student motivation in a high school earth science course, *Education Technology Research Development,* 55 169-192.

Ward, A. P. and Murray, L.W., (1985). Factors affecting performance of New Mexico high school students. Paper presented at the Meeting of the Rocky Mountain Educational Research Association, Las Cruces. (Eric Document Reproduction Service No. 271 266).

Waters, T. J., & Marzano, R. J. (2006). School district leadership that works: The effect of superintendent leadership on student achievement. Mid-Continent Research for Education and Learning. Retrieved from ERIC (ED494270).

Watkins, M. W., Lei, P.W., & Canivez, G. L. (2007). Psychometric intelligence and achievement: A cross-lagged panel analysis. *Intelligence, 35*(1), 59-68.

Weaver-Hightower, M. (2003). The 'boy turn' in research on gender and education. *Review of Educational Research, 73*(4), 471–498.

Wechler, D. (1958) *The measurement and appraisal of adult intelligence* (4th ed.) Baltemore: Williams and Wilkins.

Wei L. S. & Elias H. (2011), Relationship between students perceptions of classroom environment and their motivation in learning English language. *International Journal of Humanities and social science.* Vol. 1, 21.

Weinstein, C. S. (1992). *Designing the instructional environment: Focus on seating.* Bloomington, IN: Proceedings of Selected Research and Development Presentations at the Convention of the Association for Educational Communications and Technology. (ERIC Document Reproduction Service No. ED 348 039.

Welsh, W. N. (2000). The effect of school climate on school disorder. *Annals of the American Academy of Political and Social Sciences,* 567, 88 –107.

Wentzel, K. R. (1993). Does being good make the grade? Social behavior and academic competence in middle school, *Journal of Educational Psychology,* 85, 357-364.

Wentzel, K. R. (1994). Relations of social goal pursuit to social acceptance, classroom behavior, and perceived social support. *Journal of Educational Psychology,* 86, 173-182.

Williams, P. (1980) Adolescent identification and academic achievement: reporting the awareness of similarity to role models, *Journal of Youth and Adolescence,* 9(4), 315–321.

Williams, T. (1987). *Participation in Education.* Hawthorn: Australian Council for Educational Research.

F

G

H

I

L

M

N

O

P